**REVOL
CU**

CW00362024

The streets are ours!

Contents

www.RATB.co.uk

First edition published 2001
Second edition published 2008
This edition published 2021

ISBN 978-0-905400-30-3
Written and designed by **Rock Around the Blockade**, a campaign of the Revolutionary Communist Group. Cover image credited to Granma.cu

A brief history of Cuba

from Columbus to Batista

After Christopher Columbus claimed Cuba for Spain in 1492, the Spanish invasion led to the extermination of Cuba's indigenous population of some 100,000; through slaughter, disease and mass suicide, they were virtually wiped out within a hundred years. The Spanish then shipped slaves from Africa to labour on their sugar and tobacco plantations. By 1827, 50% of the population of Cuba was black; 40% were slaves.

Brutal treatment of slaves and discrimination against free Cubans and Criollos (Cuban-born people of Spanish origin) brought them together in revolutionary uprisings against Spanish colonial rule. In 1868 plantation owner Carlos Manuel de Cespedes freed his slaves and launched a ten-year-long liberation war throughout the less developed central and eastern parts of the island. The Spanish were finally forced to abolish slavery in Cuba in 1886. The struggle against racism in Cuba has been integral to the fight for national liberation from the outset.

Cuba's national hero, Jose Marti, who had been exiled in 1871 for his involvement in the war, built support in the United States amongst fellow Cuban exiles and émigrés. In 1895, with Antonio Maceo and Maximo Gomez, veterans of the previous war, he launched a new war of liberation. Marti was killed in battle that year, but Maceo and Gomez led a march westward from Oriente that ignited the whole island. The Spanish forces retaliated by herding the Cuban population into concentration camps where nearly 200,000 died of disease and malnutrition. Even this could not crush the independence forces.

In 1898 the US intervened and snatched victory from the Cubans. The US asserted its hegemony to 'protect' the region against the Spanish under the Monroe Doctrine of 1823, which claimed the whole of the Americas as a US sphere of influence, to the exclusion of other imperialist powers. Following the example of Britain in Egypt, the US government passed the Platt Amendment in 1901, which turned Cuba into a neo-colony and legalised US military intervention. Cuba's sovereignty and its control of foreign policy were curtailed and it was forced to sell or lease part of its territory for two US naval bases. US forces still occupy the base at Guantanamo Bay, using it as a torture camp for prisoners of the 'war on terror'.

Cuba has always been of central importance for US strategic interests in the Caribbean and Panama Canal region. To ensure its compliance and to crush rebellion, US marines returned to Cuba in 1906 to 1909 and 1912. Fearing the example of the Russian Revolution, the US returned again from 1917 to 1923, and then imposed a series of stooge pro-US presidents. From 1925 to 1933, Cuban dictator Gerardo Machado, nicknamed 'The Butcher', served US interests. But he was ousted by a mass movement leading to the revolution of 1933, which installed a progressive nationalist government. The US manoeuvred to crush this with the help of army sergeant Fulgencio Batista, who later became President. The island became a playground for wealthy US tourists during the inter-war prohibition years, taking advantage of unrestricted access to alcohol and gambling. The Mafia followed, bringing drug-trafficking and prostitution. By the 1950s, US economic interests were dominant: US companies owned two thirds of arable land, 90% of telephone and electric services, half the sugar production and virtually all mineral production, including oil, and were taking vast profits out of Cuba.

The Cuban Revolution

Moncada to Havana

Batista lost the presidency in elections in 1944, but in 1952 he returned to power with a military coup. Fidel Castro, already renowned as an anti-corruption lawyer and leading member of the radical reformist Orthodox Party, became convinced that bourgeois methods of struggle were futile. When leaders of existing political parties proved unwilling to throw out Batista, Fidel developed what was to become the 26 July Movement. On 26 July 1953, 160 young militants, most of them workers, attacked the Moncada Barracks in Santiago and the Bayamo Barracks in Oriente. Among them were Fidel and his younger brother Raul Castro. Half of the rebels were shot or tortured to death; many were imprisoned.

The leadership of the then Communist Party, *Partido Socialista Popular* (PSP) denounced the attack as putschist. Raul later responded, 'It was not a putsch designed to score an easy victory without the masses. It was a surprise action to disarm the enemy and arm the people, with the aim of beginning armed revolutionary action...it marked the start of an action to transform Cuba's entire political, economic and social system and put an end to the foreign oppression, poverty, unemployment, ill-health and ignorance that weighed upon our country and our people'.

In the trial of those who survived capture and torture, Fidel conducted his own legal defence with a ringing denunciation of the US-Batista regime and a manifesto for popular national revolution, later published as *History Will Absolve Me*. He identified three principal social forces that would determine the outcome of the revolutionary struggle:

1.the big landowners and multinational corporations represented by Batista;
2.the national bourgeoisie, among whom only the most progressive would support a revolution;

3.the masses, 'the 600,000 Cubans without work...; the 500,000 farm labourers who live in miserable shacks, who work four months of the year and starve the rest...; the 400,000 industrial workers...whose future is a pay reduction and dismissal...; the 100,000 small farmers who live and die working land that is not theirs...These are the people, the ones who know misfortune and, therefore, are capable of fighting with limitless courage'.

At that time the average annual income of the largely rural population was $91.25 – an eighth of that of Mississippi, the poorest state in the US. Only 11% of rural Cubans drank milk, 4% ate meat, 2-3% had running water and 9% had electricity. 36% of the population had intestinal parasites, 14% had tuberculosis and 43% were illiterate. A third of the workforce was totally or semi-unemployed. Life expectancy was 59 years and infant mortality was 60 per 1,000 live births. Despite this, a tiny Cuban elite enjoyed millionaire lifestyles in Havana. Without doubt there was a case for revolutionary change in Cuba.

A national movement to free the survivors of Moncada forced Batista to release Fidel and his comrades in May 1955. Fidel faced censorship and assassination threats and went to Mexico to prepare for the revolutionary armed struggle. There he met the Argentinian doctor, Ernesto 'Che' Guevara.

On 25 November 1956 the tiny yacht *Granma* left Mexico for Cuba carrying 82 revolutionaries. A simultaneous uprising planned for Santiago was crushed before the yacht could land. Batista's forces attacked the expeditionaries. A small number of survivors regrouped in the mountains of the Sierra Maestra, where the peasants and rural workers helped build the guerrilla forces, becoming the core of the Rebel Army. Essential support was provided from nearby Santiago where Frank Pais led the urban struggle. The revolution combined guerrilla warfare and mass working class struggle in the cities, united under the leadership of the 26 July Movement.

Workers' sections organised by the 26 July Movement combined industrial action with sabotage, despite the twin threats of unemployment and violent repression. The state was assisted in its repression by the Confederation of Cuban Workers trade union leadership, which had been conducting a murderous purge of communists and other radicals in the late 1940s. Civic strikes turned major Cuban cities into ghost towns. Sugar workers burned fields; telephone workers cut wires as they walked out on strike; railway workers in Guantanamo developed 'war trade unionism', combining strikes with bombings and derailings; and telephone operators listened in on police conversations to support

the armed struggles in the mountains and urban underground.

Che Guevara described the guerrilla war as one of 'constant mobility, constant distrust, and constant vigilance. What followed then was a nomadic stage in which the Rebel Army went about conquering zones of influence. It could not remain in them very long, but neither could the enemy army... various battles established a vaguely defined front between the two sides.' Within the liberated areas the Rebel Army distributed land and food supplies and issued its own laws and justice system.

The 26 July Movement, the PSP and the Revolutionary Directorate of student radicals organised uprisings and sabotage in the cities to complement the Rebel Army's actions. Following the Revolutionary Directorate's attack on the Presidential Palace in March 1957, communists were prohibited from public service, forcing them underground and into the armed struggle. On 30 July 1957, Frank Pais was captured and shot dead, aged just 23. His funeral was attended by 60,000 workers and provoked a general strike. The regime killed an estimated 20,000 people during the struggle, the majority of them active in the urban movement.

In August 1958, with Raul holding northern Oriente province, Fidel sent Rebel Army commanders Che and Camilo Cienfuegos west towards Havana. Their task was to seize Cuba's central provinces, destroying the entire political-military apparatus of the state, replacing it with new revolutionary institutions. Two small columns crossed the plains of Camaguey, finally arriving at Las Villas, cutting the island in half. By the end of December, Che's forces had seized control of the city of Santa Clara in the centre of the island, and Fidel's troops were ready to enter Santiago in the east. The regime was in crisis.

Batista fled Havana at 2am on 1 January 1959; a military junta replaced him. Fidel entered Santiago and took over the Moncada barracks. Camilo and Che led their guerrilla columns into Havana. The country was paralysed as workers and peasants responded to Fidel's call for a complete general strike in support of the revolution. At the head of the Rebel Army, Fidel's triumphant journey through the island was greeted by hundreds of thousands of cheering Cubans. He entered Havana on 8 January to proclaim that the revolution would continue.

- 3 -
Building socialism
from 1959 to the Special Period

From national democratic to socialist revolution

The new government moved quickly to improve living conditions for the Cuban people and to direct the economy in their favour. In March 1959 the Cuban Telephone Company, an affiliate of the US company ITT, was taken over and rates reduced. Medicine prices were cut and a road building programme started. Casinos were taken over and used for schools and other socially useful purposes. Opportunities for education and training were made available to those who had been drawn into the sec industry. The expansion of state education and the nationalisation of the private schools began, followed in 1961 by the astounding literacy campaign which eradicated illiteracy in Cuba within a year. In May 1959 the First Agrarian Reform Law expropriated all estates over 1,000 acres, many of them owned by US companies, and distributed land to small farmers and landless rural workers. The Urban Reform Act halved rents and forbade speculation. Those who lived in the countryside were given the houses in which they lived. By October 1960 the government had nationalised 85% of all industry and all US companies in Cuba, taken over the credit and transport systems and established a centralised planning board to oversee the transformation of the economy.

The revolutionary forces in 1959 were a multi-class alliance, united in wanting to end dictatorship and underdevelopment in Cuba. The middle classes and bourgeoisie believed Cuba's economic stagnation could be solved by technical and administrative reforms. They did not accept that Cuba's problems were determined by its status as a neo-colony. Consequently, they were unprepared for the retaliation by the United States that followed these early reforms. They saw their own interests threatened and felt the revolution was going 'too far'. Many of these people left Cuba in the first years and some became enemies of the revolution. The communists and revolutionaries understood that the social gains of the revolution could only be defended by ending imperialist domination and this in turn could only be accomplished by moving forward to building socialism. Fidel Castro later explained: 'The anti-imperialist, socialist revolution could only be one single revolution, because there is only one revolution. That is the great dialectic of humanity: imperialism and, standing against it, socialism'. So it was that the socialist nature of the revolution was proclaimed on in April 1961 as the US-backed invasion force was heading for the Bay of Pigs in south-west Cuba.

Soviet Union supports Cuba

The Cubans faced immense obstacles to building socialism. The majority of the population was desperately poor and uneducated. There was massive unemployment and virtually no health care or other social services for the bulk of the population, especially outside the cities. The people had been subject to brutal oppression and years of anti-communist propaganda. The majority of professionals, engineers and technicians had left the country. The economy relied overwhelmingly on sugar, and the main market, the United States, cancelled Cuba's sugar quota in July 1960. Above all, the United States was openly hostile to Cuba, backing terrorism and sabotage, enforcing the blockade and turning other governments against Cuba.

Fortunately, Cuba found a friend and ally in the Soviet Union. The Soviet Union exchanged oil for the bulk of Cuba's sugar at substantially higher than world market prices. The Soviet Union provided weapons, technical and military assistance and acted as a bulwark against imperialist aggression. Relations between the two countries were sometimes troubled, since their concepts of how to build socialism and how to support national liberation struggles globally were often at odds and Cuba was determined to maintain an independent path. Cuba disagreed when in 1962 Soviet premier Khrushchev capitulated to US threats and removed Soviet nuclear missiles from the island in the aftermath of the 1962 Cuban Missile Crisis. However, the Cubans have always been adamant that the support of the Soviet Union was crucial to the survival of the Cuban revolution.

Tasks and principles of the revolution

The main tasks facing the revolution were:

1. to provide everyone with the basic necessities for a dignified life – education, health care, jobs, pensions, social security. No-one in Cuba was to be abandoned to cope alone;

2. to side with the poorest and most oppressed sections of the Cuban population and to raise their political consciousness and involvement with the revolutionary process
3. to defend Cuba against imperialist aggression and threats to the revolution, both internal and external.

To fund this programme economic growth was required. For the Cuban communists, however, building socialism had to mean more than material improvements. Socialism is a transitional stage to communism, a society where the selfish, competitive and alienating relationships of capitalism are eradicated. Marx had pointed out: 'The revolution is necessary, therefore, not only because the ruling class cannot be overthrown in any other way, but also because the class overthrowing it can only in a revolution succeed in ridding itself of all the muck of ages and become fit to found society anew.'

Che Guevara argued that changing the old attitudes, or consciousness, could not be postponed until the economy had been developed. Changing people's values and the way they relate to each other and to their society is an integral part of building socialism. Building a socialist economy and socialist consciousness go together. Che wrote: 'A socialist economy without communist moral values does not interest me. We fight poverty but we also fight alienation. If communism neglects facts of consciousness, it can serve as a method of distribution but it will no longer express revolutionary moral values.'

A socialist economic programme, therefore, cannot be built with 'the rusty tools of capitalism' – commodities, competition, the pursuit of profit and the anarchy of market forces. Che argued for a centrally planned economy where each economic sector, factory and farm was allotted resources, and in return contributed to the planned requirements of the whole of society, not just its own. Through his role directing the Department of Industrialisation and Ministry of Industries, Che developed the 'Budgetary Finance System', a unique economic management system which was an alternative to the 'Auto-Financing System' used in the Soviet Union and socialist bloc. The Auto-Financing System was also used by other ministries in Cuba. This led to the 'Great Debate' between proponents of the alternative systems in Cuba. Increased productivity was encouraged, not by cut-throat economic competition between factories but by emulation: that is by comradely rivalry, each striving to surpass others in bringing benefits to the society of which they were part. Emulation was also used in preference to material incentives among individual workers. Voluntary labour, unpaid work over and above one's normal job, was another means of encouraging a socialist attitude to work. Che Guevara believed voluntary labour served to forge a sense of personal fulfilment from being part of the new society, the new world, which workers were helping to build. He said: 'This is a form of education that improves youth cadre, that prepares them for communism: the form of education in which work loses the category of obsession that it has in the capitalist world and becomes a social duty, carried out with joy, carried out with revolutionary songs, in the most fraternal camaraderie, by means of invigorating and uplifting human contact.'

Problems of bureaucracy and privilege

Capitalist countries need a bureaucracy, a layer of official workers from the middle classes and upper working class who support the system for the bourgeoisie and receive privileges in return. A privileged bureaucracy had arisen in many socialist countries as well and had become an obstacle to building socialism. The Cuban communists sought to prevent that happening in Cuba. The working class had taken power and it had no need for a separate, privileged layer of administrators. The Cubans cut the numbers of officials and their privileges, instructing them to work in co-operation with, and not separately from, the rest of the workforce. Workers and management planned together. New officials and administrators were recruited from the working class. Whilst huge steps were made, bureaucracy remains an issue and tackling it has been a repeated theme of debate in Cuba.

Following the departure of Che Guevara from Cuba in 1965, the revolutionary state continued to change and adapt its economic management system. Problems were demonstrated by the failures of the 1970 '10 million tonne harvest'. The economy was distorted as whole sectors were shut down and other agricultural production neglected in order to meet the ambitious target, a heroic effort which ultimately fell short. Consequently, in an effort to restore order over the economy, in the 1970s the Cubans adopted the Soviet economic model. Under this model each productive unit had a great deal of autonomy, traded with other units, operated on a profit and loss basis and paid taxes similarly to capitalist enterprises. Management dominated decision-making and encouraged productivity through bonuses, which state enterprises kept for themselves. As these ideas took hold in Cuba, an entrenched bureaucracy began to develop. Corruption grew and socialist consciousness stagnated. Cynicism and self-interest threatened the revolution. Again the

Communist Party took steps to remedy the situation. In 1986 it launched a rectification campaign – a penetrating self-criticism of the revolution's progress. Fidel Castro pointed to Che's critique of the Soviet system to explain the problems that had emerged. Private markets were closed, non-material incentives were encouraged and voluntary work brigades established to construct housing and day-care centres for children.

A revolution of the working class

Such timely interventions were possible because the Communist Party had made close ties with the people its top priority, involving them in the revolutionary process and raising their political consciousness. From the earliest days, Fidel and his comrades spoke with the people directly at mass rallies, on television and radio, visiting workplaces and participating in neighbourhood meetings.

The people's militias were formed in 1959. These enabled millions of Cubans to be trained in the armed defence of their revolution. Soon after mass organisations were created to mobilise the working class such as Committees for the Defence of the Revolution (CDRs), the Federation of Cuban Women (FMC), the National Association of Small Farmers (ANAP) and the Union of Young Communists (UJC). It is largely through involvement in the mass organisations that Cubans participate in the revolutionary transformation of Cuba. Through participation comes the political consciousness essential to all revolutionaries. The establishment of *Poder Popular* (Popular Power) in the 1970s marked a further step towards the total involvement of the people with their revolution (see chapter 6). Decision-making was put into the hands of the people so that, in the words of Fidel, 'the revolutionary process may become a formidable school of government in which millions of people will learn to take on responsibilities and resolve problems of government'.

In 1975 a draft constitution was debated across the island, amended

and adopted by popular referendum in 1976. It affirmed the leading role of the Cuban Communist Party. No-one can simply choose to join the Party. Members are recommended by their neighbours or work colleagues on the basis of their commitment and socialist consciousness. In this way the chances of self-seeking careerists entering the Party are reduced. The purpose of the Communist Party is not to run the state. Its main role is ideological. It maintains a close relationship with the working class and tries to ensure that ideas are applied creatively to specific conditions. The mass organisations are the 'arms and legs' of the Communist Party, the means by which the people are organised and mobilised. The Party submits documents for discussion to the National Assembly of People's Power or for nationwide consultation, but ultimately it is the people through referendums and the National Assembly, that decide the key policies of Cuba.

The Special Period

Without this bond between Party and people, without the years of struggle and participation in the revolution that built up the Cuban people's political consciousness, the Cuban revolution would have failed when the Soviet Union and the socialist countries of Eastern Europe collapsed in 1989–91. Cuba suddenly lost over 85% of its markets and most of its oil supply. In the next three years, Gross Domestic Product (GDP) fell by 34% and imports by over 75%. The situation was made considerably worse by an intensification of the US blockade, falling sugar prices and rising oil prices. Just about everything was in short supply. There were severe reductions in subsidised food, rising unemployment, frequent cuts in power and water supplies and shortages of medicines and basic goods. The Cuban transport system virtually ground to a halt. Social programmes, such as the building of crèches and housing, had to be halted for lack of construction materials.

Cuba was not, however, taken by surprise. The Cuban Communist Party had seen how market-style reforms in the Soviet Union were leading down the capitalist road and, in the late 1980s, Fidel had warned of the possible demise of the Soviet Union. He now declared this was a Special Period for Cuba and measures would be introduced to safeguard the revolution.

The government put emergency plans into operation. It introduced joint ventures with capitalist foreign enterprises to restart some industries and expand tourism to get badly needed hard currency, needed to buy imports on the international market. It legalised possession of dollars and opened special dollar shops selling scarce and luxury items. It extended oil and mineral exploration and introduced imaginative solutions to help solve shortages in transport and agriculture. Everywhere economic efficiency was tightened. The army was employed in food production. Further rationing was introduced. State land was made available for collective cultivation and self-employment was permitted to help ease unemployment.

These measures inevitably generated new contradictions within socialist Cuba. For instance, Cuban workers in the tourist industry had ready access to dollars. A waiter could gain as much from one tip as a teacher or doctor earned in a week. Farmers at private markets were free to sell their produce at raised prices. Inequalities among the Cuban people increased. Those with dollars had privileged access to goods and services. In the wake of the expansion of tourism, crime and prostitution increased. The government took steps to counteract these problems. Taxes were introduced for those with access to dollar incomes via self-employment. To reduce inequalities, tourist workers were encouraged to donate half their tips to social projects and, as conditions allowed, prices were reduced and more Cubans given access to dollars at special rates of exchange. However, these problems could not be eradicated entirely because the Cubans were partly relying on market mechanisms and the international market to rebuild their economy.

The main battle of the Special Period was therefore political and ideological: to maintain socialist consciousness and unity among the people under the pressure of the capitalist market and imperialist aggression. The response of the Cuban Communist Party was to strengthen its connection with the working class. Every problem was discussed with the people; every measure open to scrutiny and amendment; every political consequence explained. Despite the enormous economic difficulties, not a single school, hospital or old people's home was closed. Unemployed workers were maintained on 60% of their wages and retrained until they could be employed again. Fidel Castro and the Cuban state made difficult political decisions to protect Cubans from the shock therapy that the former Soviet bloc was subjected to. Official prices, wages and the exchange rate were fixed, health care and education spending were maintained, subsidies for basic goods were increased, employment levels were maintained even when productivity fell to rock bottom. Scarcity of fuel meant frequent planned blackouts, as electricity for hospitals and other essential services were prioritised. Calorie consumption dropped by a third, although the ration system ensured that no-one starved, and children continued to receive daily milk.

Economically, life began to improve, though still not to a point where the Cubans could remove the distortions of the capitalist market and resume the building of a socialist economy. For much of this period growth was kept above 5% per year, and it peaked at 13% in 2006. This has to be compared with 1% to 3% GDP growth rates in most other Latin American and Western countries. In the year 2000, 124,000 new jobs were created and since then, there have been increases in workers' wages and pensions. The house building programme was restarted, running at 70,000 a year, and there was a major expansion of education, with universities opened in every municipality. Most important of all, the Cubans have maintained an independent economic and financial policy. They are not in debt to the IMF nor subject to its neo-liberal austerity packages. When compared to the slashing and privatisation prevalent in capitalist societies in crisis, Cuba's response to severe economic crisis is astounding; a feat of socialist planning and popular mobilisation.

4

Cuban socialism into the 21st century

Events at the turn of the century propelled Cuba to once again investigate and address the contradictions and challenges the Special Period had produced, galvanising the economy and mobilising the population.

The battle for Elian

In November 1999, Elian Gonzalez, a six-year-old Cuban child, was found adrift at sea after his mother had taken him without his father's permission, and left Cuba by boat. Elian's mother had died on the journey and the US Immigration and Naturalization Service gave custody of Elian to distant relatives in Miami, right-wing members of the exile community.

Elian's father appealed to Fidel Castro for help. Fidel responded by staking the prestige of the revolution on a legal and political campaign to return Elian to Cuba. The rich and powerful Cuban exile community, among them Congresswoman Ileana Ros-Lehtinen and Miami-Dade County Mayor Alex Penelas, refused to release Elian, ignoring the Federal Authority's demand that the child be returned to his father in line with international law.

In Cuba, the demand to return Elian prompted mass grassroots mobilisation on a scale not seen since the early 1960s, as millions of people, including schoolchildren, took to the streets in protest. It became an international campaign. Finally, on 22 April 2000, US border agents seized Elian from his Miami relatives and reunited him with his father who was waiting for him in the US. They returned to Cuba on 28 June 2000.

While in the US, Elian's father, a member of the Cuban Communist Party, was offered millions of dollars to defect and stay with his son in Miami, but he refused. Afterwards, he received no material rewards for his loyalty, continuing in his job as a waiter. Today, Elian plays a key role in his local community, leading his neighbourhood CDR and became a member of the Cuban Communist Party in 2020.

Che Guevara: 1928 to 1967
an outline of his revolutionary life and ideas

Ernesto 'Che' Guevara was born into a radical middle-class family in Argentina in 1928. He grew up reading despatches from the Spanish Civil War written by his uncle, a member of the Argentinian Communist Party. During and after his medical studies he toured Latin America, witnessing the appalling poverty, marginalisation, hunger and disease suffered by the mass of people. He refused to accept that such a state was a natural and unchangeable purgatory for humanity and began searching for solutions.

In 1954 he was in Guatemala where a progressive government was redistributing land nationalised from the United Fruit Company. In response, then US President Eisenhower and the CIA backed an invasion and counter-revolution that killed thousands of people. Forced into exile, frustrated by the Guatemalan government's refusal to distribute arms and defend the gains made, Che was convinced of the necessity of armed struggle and left for Mexico. There, he read Marx, Lenin and books on military strategy and met up with the Cuban revolutionaries preparing for the Granma expedition. Che was immediately recruited as the expedition's doctor.

Once they had landed in Cuba, Che had to choose between his duties as a doctor and those as a revolutionary: 'At my feet were a pack of medicines and a cartridge box; together they were too heavy to carry. I chose the cartridge box...' Despite suffering from severe asthma, he became an outstanding guerrilla leader of the Cuban revolution and subsequently one of its foremost political leaders.

After the revolution, Che volunteered to take on the most difficult tasks. He headed the newly formed Department of Industrialisation, became President of the National Bank and later Minister of Industries, all within two years. He thus became immersed in the development of the Cuban economy, industrialisation, and the political education of the working class and peasantry to defend their revolution and begin the transition to socialism.

Che's internationalism — 'to fight against imperialism wherever it may be' — propelled him to leave Cuba and join the struggle in the Congo in April 1965. In November 1966 he attempted to open a new guerrilla front in Bolivia. He was captured by the Bolivian army on 8 October 1967 and executed the next day.

Che's message lives on. In tribute to him after his death, Fidel Castro said that, 'our fighters, our revolutionaries, our Party members, our children', should strive to be like Che, 'because Che is the personification, the image of that new person, is the image of that human being if we want to talk about a communist society'.

Che's image is recognised throughout the world as a romantic icon, but this demeans him. Che was first and foremost a communist, a Marxist-Leninist and a revolutionary. He wrote extensively on politics, economics and the role of the working class. His ideas on what it means to build socialism have been, and will increasingly become, a powerful weapon in the battle for a new society.

The Battle of Ideas

Fidel then urged a profound analysis of the circumstances which had led Elian's mother, and thousands like her, to risk their lives to leave the island. Cubans emigrate to the US for the same economic reasons that millions of Latin Americans do: in search of material improvements. But having survived the hardships of the Special Period, Cuba was now in a position to begin re-evaluating its achievements and errors, as Fidel said: 'to develop a critical rather than self-indulgent vision of our undertaking and our historical objectives.' This was the 'Battle of Ideas': education and culture were key tools to create commitment to political ideas, but these would be abstract if the standard of living didn't alleviate daily concerns for survival.

The first step was to analyse the situation of the entire Cuban population. Within two months student volunteers had surveyed the weight and height of every Cuban child under 17, mapping out areas of malnutrition. A similar campaign followed for pensioners. It was discovered that there was a section of young people between 16 and 20 who had not achieved the grades to enter further education, nor did they have employment. This section was potentially marginalised from the revolution, not participating in work or study-based organisations, not contributing to social progress, nor experiencing its benefits.

Social workers

These teenagers were given the opportunity to become social workers in their own communities. During an intensive course studying a range of topics, they worked with their neighbours to assess the socio-economic issues which affected them. Such was the success of the programme that by the start of 2006 there were 28,000 social workers, with an average age of 18. By 2007 there were more than 7,000 projects initiated as part of the Battle of Ideas: constructing schools to reduce class sizes; adult education courses and technical training; new medical and therapeutic facilities; video and computer clubs; solar panel-powered provision of TV, video and computers in every rural school.

The aim was to 'create a society that is increasingly more just, more egalitarian, more humane in every area and dimension... creating new challenges, new objectives and new hopes for all those who have the privilege of being born on Cuban soil.' It represented an ideological battle for the soul of the revolution, uniting the Cuban population to emerge stronger from the harsh conditions of the Special Period.

Updating the Cuban economy

Next there came a drive to improve the economy. In 2006 Fidel Castro's health deteriorated and he retired. Raul Castro was elected President of the Council of State in his place. In 2007 the Cuban government created forums for everyone in the country to contribute to a 'Great Debate' about Cuba's socio-economic problems and to suggest concrete solutions. The survival of Cuban socialism required an urgent increase in national income, the elimination of a balance of payments deficit and import substitution. Capital was needed to rebuild infrastructure, update technology and raise productivity to improve wages and standards of living. As a small blockaded Caribbean island without sufficient savings, Cuba needed to rely on Foreign Direct Investment, aiming to attract $2 to £2.5bn a year, while finding ways to productively use the estimated $3bn in remittances that enters the island each year.

The Guidelines of the Social and Economic Policy of the Party and the Revolution were compiled, with proposals to address the issues raised. These Guidelines were circulated for six months of public consultation prior to the 6th Congress of the Cuban Communist Party in April 2011. After nearly nine million Cubans debated the draft, 68% of the proposals were modified before being submitted to the National Assembly for approval. This formidable democratic process legitimised the programme to improve economic efficiency and productive capacity within a socialist framework.

Rejecting claims that Cuba is returning to capitalism, the introduction to the Guidelines affirmed, 'only socialism is capable of overcoming the difficulties and preserving the conquests of the Revolution, and that in the updating of the economic model, planning will be supreme, not the market'.

These measures, designed to enable long-term sustainable socialist development, included the handing over of idle land in usufruct (rent-free usage) to farmers and co-operatives, the transfer of workers from the state to the non-state sector, new labour codes, new tax codes, the creation of experimental non-agricultural co-operatives and new forms of self-employment. Foreign investment was geared towards boosting Cuban exports and producing goods for domestic consumption. To this end, in 2014, the Mariel Port and Special Economic Development Zone were inaugurated and a new foreign investment law approved. State enterprises still produce 85% of products; foreign direct investment is encouraged but with the Cuban state usually maintaining a majority controlling stake.

Accompanying the implementation of these measures, two further key documents were discussed and adopted in 2017, setting out the direction of the updates to the economy: Conceptualisation of the Economic and Social Model of Cuban Socialist Development and Basis for the Plan of Economic and Social Development up till 2030: Vision of the Nation, Axes and Strategic Sectors (Plan 2030). Accordingly, these documents also went through a collective process of writing, analysis, modification and approval: Raul Castro described them as 'the most studied, discussed and re-discussed documents in the history of the Revolution'.

One of the objectives of the economic reforms has been to increase productivity in order to raise salaries and reunify the currency, a process which began in January 2021. Prior to this, Cuba had two currencies; the national peso (CUP), and the convertible peso (CUC), which was introduced in 1994 during the Special Period, to restrict and remove the circulation of the US dollar. State salaries were typically paid in the national peso whilst the CUC was primarily used for joint enterprises and tourism. Most luxury imported goods like laptops and mobile phones were sold in CUC. The value of the CUC was fixed to the US dollar and exchangeable for around 25 CUP. The dual currency was important to get Cuba through the Special Period and US aggression, but it created serious distortions in the Cuban economy. Although the Cuban government declared the long term goal of currency reunification in 2013, the process demanded careful preparation to protect the value of savings, income and the cost of products for the population..

Rejuvenation of the leadership

Raul Castro stepped down as President in 2018 after two terms in office; he will remain as leader of the Communist Party until 2021. A new president, Miguel Diaz-Canel Bermudez, was elected in 2018, the first leader of Cuba's government born after the 1959 revolution. Of those elected to the Council of State, 42% were new members, 48% are women, and 45% are black or mixed race. Of the six Vice Presidents elected, three are black, including the First Vice President Salvador Valdes Mesa, and three are women. 77% of the Council of State were born after the 1959 revolution. Through these elections, the average age of deputies was reduced from 57 to 49 years old, with the youngest being 19. This represents a systematic effort to rejuvenate the leadership of the revolution, ensuring its continuation across generations.

Fidel Castro 1926 – 2016
Changing everything that needs to be changed

Fidel Castro, Commander in Chief of the Cuban Revolution, served the global anti-imperialist struggle until his death in 2016 aged 90. Despite hundreds of assassination attempts against him following the victory of the Cuban Revolution in January 1959, he died a natural death in peace in Havana, having seen off nine hostile US Presidents.

Fidel's genius was his ability to meet the need for tactical steps, responding to the day's urgencies, without losing sight of the strategic direction – the revolutionary principles – that have driven Cuba's progress. In the 1950s, Fidel set out the Moncada Programme, risking his life on the front line in Cuba's revolutionary armed struggle against the Batista dictatorship.

Fidel set out on the hardest possible path of building the greatest possible involvement of all the population in the Revolution's tasks. There were failures, which were addressed publicly in the spirit of self-criticism. Today, participatory democracy, 'People's Power', is at the heart of Cuban society, 'from below' at every level: neighbourhood, community, regional and national.

Fidel's voice could not be silenced. His famous address to the United Nations in 1960 condemned the injustices of imperialism and colonialism. He committed Cuba to support revolutionary movements across the world, hosting the Tricontinental Conference to co-ordinate anti-imperialist forces internationally. After his release from 27 years in prison in 1990, Nelson Mandela prioritised a visit to Havana to thank Fidel Castro for Cuba's role in defeating apartheid: 'What other country can point to a record of greater selflessness than Cuba has displayed in its relations to Africa?' Mandela said.

In the 1980s Fidel called for the cancellation of unpayable Third World debt. In the 1990s he stood with the victims of the rapacious multinationals and global corporations supported by the IMF and World Trade Organisation, exposing the genocidal results of neo-liberal policies, and warning the world about the ecological crisis which threatened humanity and the planet. Through the 2000s Fidel guided Cuba's internationalist principles and the idea of production and exchange determined by need, not profit. Under his leadership Cuba emerged as a nation with outstanding human development indices in health, education, sport and culture, with a globally recognised record of international solidarity and a model of ecological sustainability.

Of these important contributions by Fidel and the Cuban Revolution, little has been spoken in the mainstream media. We are not surprised that on his death, Fidel was not forgiven the 'crime' of building socialism and continues to be lambasted as a dictator. We understand this diatribe for what it is: fear. Fear of the example of a great revolutionary leader, who spoke up for the poor and oppressed, who showed that principles do not weaken with age, and showed us that another world is possible. That world is socialist.

The non-state sector and co-operatives

The non-state sector has grown as part of the economic programme to update the Cuban economy, addressing distortions from the Special Period where unemployed workers were maintained on state salaries despite the closure of industries and many workplaces. As of 2019, Cuba had a work force of 4.6 million, with over 3 million in the state sector and 1.4 million in the non-state sector which includes cooperatives, private farmers, usufruct farmers, the self-employed and small businesses. Remittances - money sent by family members

abroad - have injected cash into this sector, which benefits the state via higher taxation which is invested in the social system as a whole. Both self-employed enterprises and co-operatives can now hire other self-employed workers under contract and wages are typically much higher in the non-state sector.

In addition to monetary wages, the Cuban state provides health care, education and access to sport and culture for free for everyone, and heavily subsidises basic necessities including food, housing, transportation, gas and electricity. Therefore, wages in Cuba do not determine whether you can afford to eat or pay rent as they do under capitalism. Though there have been significant salary increases across the state sector since 2014, a rebalancing of wages between the state and non-state sector is essential in order to guarantee the long-term stability of the economy and state provision of public services.

Since 2012, non-agricultural co-operatives have been promoted as a more collective model within the non-state sector. They are playing a key role in the economic drive for efficiency, with cooperatives running taxis and some sectors of transport, repairing and maintaining state-owned vehicles, producing textiles and clothing, running restaurants and repairing buildings, among other activities. The management committee is elected by the workforce and holds workers' general assemblies to inspect finances and performance and make collective decisions on future plans. Cooperatives often contribute to their community by donating time and funds to local projects.

Whilst non agricultural cooperatives are relatively new, various types of co-operatives have long been a feature of Cuban agriculture. Under the direction of ANAP, the National Association of Small Agricultural Producers, these co-operatives group together associates and small private farmers in order to plan their production of food. Typically 80% of products are sold to the state with the remaining 20% for personal use and private sale. Co-operatives usually guarantee benefits like pensions or parental leave pay and some invest time and money into the local community, for example by providing materials for house construction and repair.

Increasing food production is crucial. Only 24% of Cuba's population live in rural areas. Free university education has resulted in the majority of Cubans being educated to highly qualified levels. The challenge is to encourage people to stay and work in the countryside and produce food. Higher wages in agricultural co-operatives, and collaboration with universities to promote the application of ecology and environmental science to food production are increasing youth employment in agriculture. In addition, voluntary brigades continue to be actively promoted; In 2018, in Havana alone, 2,449 young people participated in the Union of Young Communists' voluntary work brigades.

While a necessity, the increased use of market mechanisms presents challenges to the basic principles of the Cuban revolution; how do you preserve sovereignty and independence while inviting foreign investment? How do you hold in check the growth of inequality that accompanies the legalisation of the private contracting of workers by small businesses and cooperatives?

Aware of the contradictions and potential dangers, the Cuban leadership continues to carefully implement, analyse and modify the economic reforms, in step with feedback from Cuban workers and mass organisations. The urgent priority continues to be strengthening the economy in the face of increasing hostility from the US.

In 2019, Raul Castro emphasised this in a televised speech to the nation

'Efforts must be redoubled to increase domestic production, particularly food production, review all expenditures to eliminate non-essentials, increase efficiency in the use of energy, especially fuels… In 60 years against the aggressions and threats, Cubans have shown the iron will to resist and overcome the most difficult circumstances. Despite its immense power, imperialism does not possess the capacity to break the dignity of a united people, proud of its history and of the freedom conquered by so much sacrifice... We will always resist, fight and achieve victory. There is no other alternative.'

The Cuban workers are clear that increasing productivity and efficiency is defending the revolution.

5

The US blockade and aggression against Cuba

The US ruling class understands that socialist Cuba represents an alternative for the oppressed people of the world and, as such, a threat to the whole capitalist system. Consequently, it has tried every conceivable means to overthrow the Cuban revolution, from sabotage and military invasion to biological warfare and economic strangulation, even risking nuclear war in the process.

Sabotage, invasion and biological warfare

As early as 1959 the Eisenhower administration drew up a 'Program of covert operations against the Castro regime'. It trained and armed counter-revolutionary gangs operating in the Cuban countryside, who murdered young volunteers, rural workers and children taking part in the great literacy campaign. CIA agents destroyed factories, farms and fuel depots and planted bombs in cinemas and stores. Others machine-gunned coastal villages from speedboats, hijacked aircraft and attacked Cuban fishing boats. Abroad, they attacked Cuban diplomats and offices.

In March 1960, Eisenhower ordered the CIA to start training Cuban exiles in Guatemala for a full-scale invasion of Cuba. Spy flights were already taking place over Cuba. Two months later the US began propaganda broadcasts to Cuba from neighbouring countries, inciting Cubans to acts of sabotage and counter-revolution. These broadcasts have continued ever since. On 15 April 1961, the US attacked Cuba with B26 bombers, killing seven Cubans. The next day a force of 1,200 mercenaries, led by CIA agents, landed at the Bay of Pigs. It was supported by US warships, while US bombers dropped napalm and high explosives. The invasion was quickly defeated by the massive response of the Cuban people and armed forces, led personally by Fidel Castro. The planes were shot down and two ships were sunk; 176 Cubans were killed in the attack and over 300 wounded.

Cuba has been subjected to a sustained barrage of sabotage and bacteriological warfare. Between November 1961 and January 1963 alone over 5,000 acts of terrorism were carried out against Cuba. Attacks have included:

- March 1960 – US agents blew up a French armaments ship in Havana harbour, killing 101 people
- October 1962 – US President Kennedy risked a nuclear war when he imposed a naval blockade on Cuba to get Soviet missiles removed from the island
- October 1976 – *Cubana de Aviacion*, a Cuban airliner, was blown up in mid-flight. All 73 people on board were killed
- May 1981 – an epidemic of Dengue fever killed 158 people including 101 children. The particular strain of virus was brought to Cuba by Omega 7, a group of Cuban exiles based in the US.
- 1962-1994 – 13,000 acts of provocation from the US base at Guantanamo resulted in the deaths of eight Cubans
- 1997 – an Italian tourist was killed when bombs were planted in Havana hotels
- 1998 – a plague of *Thryps Palmiae*, an insect which devastates crops, was spread across Cuba by a US plane
- Cuba estimates that between 1960 and 2020, such actions by the US and its agents have cost at least 3,478 Cuban lives and incapacitated at least another 2,099 people.

Imperialist dirty tricks – manufacturing conflict

In March 1962, Operation Northwood - which specifically aimed to create 'pretexts to justify military intervention in Cuba'- was established in what is still today a strand of US strategy. The authors of the plan envisaged destroying a US warship or civilian plane in such a way that it would appear to be the result of Cuban action, providing the US with a justification to invade. Accepting that the Cuban people would not oppose the revolution, the plan relied on counter-revolutionary Cuban exiles. The saboteurs and CIA agents who attack Cuba today are still mainly drawn from the Cuban exile population. Based in Florida, the exile leadership comes chiefly from families whose criminal or privileged lifestyles were ended by the revolution and who wish to overthrow socialism so they can return to exploit the Cuban people once more.

Among the 1,000 prisoners taken at the Bay of Pigs invasion were rich Cuban exiles who before the revolution had owned nearly a million acres of land,

10,000 houses, 70 factories, five mines, two banks and ten sugar mills. Within the US, these reactionaries are organised within the Cuban American National Foundation (CANF). Known in Cuba as the 'Miami Mafia', CANF has close links with right-wing US politicians at the highest levels of government.

The US blockade

A second plank of US strategy to defeat the Cuban revolution has been the economic war. The US economic blockade was initiated by President Eisenhower in 1960 and has been progressively tightened ever since, in particular by the Cuban Democracy Act of 1992 (known as the Torricelli Act) and the Cuban Liberty and Democratic Solidarity Act of 1996 (known as the Helms-Burton Act). Both acts were sponsored by right-wing associates of CANF. Together they mean that:

- No US company or foreign subsidiary can trade with Cuba;
- No items with US-made components can be sold to Cuba;
- No Cuban goods or items with any component of Cuban origin can be sold in the United States;
- No US bank or financial institution can give credit to Cuba or support any foreign transaction with Cuba;
- Any ship that docks in Cuba cannot enter a US port for a period of at least six months;
- Any foreign company that trades with Cuba is open to retaliation by the US, which may include the banning of company directors and their families from entering the United States; US trade with any company which uses Cuban sugar products is specifically forbidden;
- The blockade cannot be lifted unless there is 'a transition to representative democracy' which would allow the US to set up a transitional government without any members of the Cuban government or Communist Party; in the 'free and fair' elections that would follow members of the Communist Party would not be allowed to stand. The US President would have the right to review the Cuban government annually and re-impose the blockade if it did not meet with their approval;
- The President must report to Congress on (and hence presumably spy upon) countries, companies and individuals who trade with Cuba.

The blockade also has many indirect consequences for Cuba. For instance, imports have to be sought further afield, at higher prices and with extra transport costs.

Products, including medicines, cannot be manufactured because the necessary ingredients or components are only made in the US. Foreign loans are more difficult to obtain and cost more to service. Foreign firms pull out of trade deals and joint ventures because of retaliatory threats by the US treasury.

In 2000, following pressure by some US farmers and agribusiness, exemptions were made to the blockade to allow the export of certain food and medical products to Cuba. However, these exports must be paid for in cash before the goods leave US ports, a difficult requirement for any country, let alone one starved of foreign currency. Since 2006 the US Treasury Department has changed export licences to prevent the sale of equipment and medicines to Cuba's most important hospitals.

Overall, the Cuban government calculates the blockade has cost Cuba over $900bn in damages and has caused an incalculable amount of human suffering. Each year since 1992 the United Nations General Assembly members vote overwhelmingly against the US blockade of Cuba. Only the US and Israel consistently vote in its favour, occasionally joined by a couple of other pressured countries.

Although the extraterritoriality of the US blockade is completely illegal in international law, Cuba solidarity work in Britain has been targeted. In 2015 PayPal blocked the accounts of Rock around Blockade's solidarity campaign because of merchandise sold to support the cause, denying the right to appeal. In 2016 Eventbrite confiscated funds raised by a classical music concert in London to send a piano to a Cuban music school.

US out of Guantanamo

Today, the US concentration camp in occupied Guantanamo is notorious. It must be closed and the land given back to Cuba. The Cuban people have always opposed this imperialist occupation, and since the 1959 revolution Cuba has demanded an end to the US presence with regular demonstrations at its gates. In protest against the occupation, Cuba refuses US offers to pay for the 'lease' of its land.

Since January 2002, as part of the so-called 'War on Terror', the US government has held 775 people without trial in a specially built concentration camp in occupied Guantanamo Bay. Inmates are allowed one to three hours' exercise a week in a caged recreation yard measuring 7.6 by 9.1 metres. Torture at the hands of US guards is systematic. In 2002 Asif Iqbal from Birmingham, who, with two of his friends, was kidnapped by imperialist forces in Afghanistan and sent to Guantanamo, described repeated interrogations, ear-splitting music, flashing lights, extreme temperatures and three months' solitary confinement. Other torture methods include electrical shocks, drowning in water tanks, depriving of food and water, chaining and hanging from the ceiling. At least nine prisoners have died.

When Barack Obama became US President, he promised to close the prison camp and in January 2009 he signed an executive order for its closure within a year. He failed to deliver on this promise and by September 2020 40 detainees still remained. Three of these men were cleared for release in 2009 by Obama's Guantanamo Review Task Force. Few have been charged with any crime and all are denied basic civil and legal rights. Against international law, the US Military Commissions Act 2006 permits indefinite detention without charge or trial and allows the holding of 'military tribunals' where defendants are not informed of and cannot challenge the evidence against them. Dozens of inmates have staged hunger strikes and other protests against their detention. Alongside US agents, British MI5 agents have been implicated in the interrogation of Guantanamo detainees.

RATB demands the release of all the detainees and for the dismantling of the US concentration camp at Guantanamo In the words of Ricardo Alarcon, former President of Cuba's National Assembly, 'this prison should be closed down immediately, and Guantanamo should be returned to its rightful owner, the people of Cuba.'

Track Two

An insidious aspect of the blockade legislation is what is known as Track Two of the Torricelli Act. This involves encouraging the creation of counter-revolutionary groups and pro-capitalist sympathies within Cuba. Under Track Two the US promotes contacts between non-governmental organisations in Cuba and the West, with the intention of developing bourgeois notions of so-called civil society among Cuban intellectuals. This was a tactic used to great effect by imperialism in the socialist countries of Eastern Europe. It is reinforced by direct funding and support for US agents in Cuba trying to form counter-revolutionary organisations, funded under US institutions and supposed foreign NGOs such as the US Agency for International Development (USAID) and the National Endowment for Democracy (NED). The US government spends $20m a year on what are effectively regime change programmes.

In May 2001 legislation was introduced into the US Senate by Jesse Helms calling for $100m to be made available to assist so-called dissidents in Cuba.

Under the guise of 'fighting human rights abuses' and 'promoting democracy', the US government funnels money to USAID to promote destabilisation in Cuba and in recent years the use of technology, including social media, has become one of its most effective political tools.

Tweets, terrorism and mercenaries

In 2009, during the US presidency of Barack Obama, Alan Gross, a private subcontractor on a $500,000 mission to install telecommunications equipment and laptops with internet access with the aim of promoting subversion, was arrested and imprisoned by Cuban authorities. Gross was working as a mercenary for US company Development Alternatives Inc which, in 2008, won a $6m contract with USAID to 'advance democracy' in Cuba. It was rumoured he was connected to US-based internet service providers. Meanwhile the US blockade prevents Cuba from accessing most of the undersea fibre-optic cables which skirt the island. Gross was sentenced to 15 years' incarceration, but was released in 2014 after serving just three, in exchange for the release of remaining three of Cuban Five who remained in US jail (see chapter 14).

Various USAID plans to 'advance democracy' in Cuba were exposed while Obama was in secret negotiations with Cuba about improving relations. Between 2009 and 2012 USAID awarded $6 million in contracts to Creative Associates to recruit a dozen young people from Peru, Venezuela and Costa Rica. They were sent to Cuba as travellers and tourists in order to 'identify potential social-change actors' and organise opposition to destabilise the Cuban government. In 2014 USAID created a fake Twitter-style programme 'ZunZuneo' with the aim of fomenting political opposition amongst Cuba's youth by sending out political material to create anti-government sentiment and encourage instigation of political protests.

The use of information technology in the war against socialism has been seen in the cultivation of 'dissident' bloggers such as Yoani Sanchez, who went from nonentity to international fame in 2008 when *Time* magazine listed her among the world's 100 most influential people, while most Cubans had never heard of her. Sanchez was catapulted to international relevance and by the following year had received over £500,000 in 'prize' money. Although Trump's 2018 budget severely cut USAID programmes, that same year the administration commissioned the creation of the Cuba Internet Task Force (CITF), to explore ways the US can exploit the expansion of internet access to reach more Cubans with regime change propaganda.

Rapprochement- the economic attack continues

Starting in 2014, US President Obama eased some of the blockade's restrictions as part of an approach of 'smart diplomacy' which sought to advance US imperialist interests through a policy of persuasion, seduction and bribery, as opposed to isolation and aggression, which had failed to achieve its objectives for over 50 years. Despite this, Cuba remained blockaded and under political pressure from US-funded initiatives. During Obama's presidency, 49 companies were fined under blockade legislation with the sanctions amounting to $14.3bn, higher than under any previous US president. Some of these companies were not even based in the United States. US administrations, regardless of who is president, consistently attack Cuba, threaten investment, obstruct trade and starve it of the revenue needed to survive. The election of President Trump in 2016 reversed Obama's small concessions to Cuba. Trump's administration returned to the kind of aggressive rhetoric not seen since the Cold War under President Ronald Reagan, with an aggressive tightening of sanctions to obstruct Cuba's income and scare off investors. In this context the Trump administration activated a long-dormant piece of anti-Cuban legislation; Title III of the Helms-Burton Act which had been suspended by every president since the Act itself was passed in 1996; it is a dramatic expansion of the US's illegal blockade. It allows lawsuits to be brought in US courts against companies (including foreign ones) that benefited from assets that Cuba nationalised after the revolution. Travel to Cuba from the US was once again restricted only to those visiting immediate family; limits on remittances were tightened.

Title III is designed to push the Cuban economy into crisis by significantly increasing the already considerable legal and financial risk for foreign investors of dealing with Cuba. Due to the financial harm it could do to companies and individuals in third countries, it added to tensions between the US and Cuba's trading partners, particularly Canada and the EU which issued a joint warning that the US would be violating international law. In 2019 and 2020, the Revolutionary Communist Group and Rock around the Blockade held pickets of Esso (ExxonMobil) to highlight its lawsuit under Title III and pledged to publicly target companies that attempt to capitalise on the expansion of the Helms-Burton Act (See Chapter 14).

The election of President Joe Biden in 2020 promised to roll back some of Trump's most vicious attacks. However successive Democrat and Republican administrations have maintained the blockade; changes in tactics are always consistent with US imperialist hostility to Cuban socialism and sovereignty.

6

British imperialism and Cuba

British governments have consistently sided with US imperialism to attack the Cuban revolution. In 1959 Britain cancelled the sale of jet fighters to Cuba. In 1960, refused to allow British Guyana to accept a Cuban loan of £5m to develop its timber industry. The loan demonstrated Cuba's internationalist solidarity with oppressed nations. Its terms were to be 10 years at 2% interest, payment to be made in timber. In 1962, less than a year after the Bay of Pigs failed mercenary invasion, Britain helped to defeat a UN resolution calling on the US to stop interfering in Cuba's affairs. The Security Council rejected the proposal with the British delegate branding Cuba's charges 'a propaganda exercise'. That same year, as the Soviet Union deployed missiles to defend Cuba against further attacks, the US imposed a naval blockade and threatened invasion leading to the October missile crisis of 1962. Supporting US plans, Britain agreed to allow the US to store military equipment at Mayaguana in the Bahamas. Nuclear war was averted after the Soviet Union agreed to remove the missiles on the condition of the US ending the naval blockade against Cuba and lifting the threat of invasion, however, CIA backed attacks on Cuba continued whilst the US maintained its economic blockade of the island.

In 1964, Britain supported these sanctions by suspending credits to British Leyland for the sale of buses to Cuba and has allowed the illegal US blockade to operate extra-territorially ever since. For instance, in 1996 The European Council adopted Regulation (EC) No. 2271/96 and the British Parliament approved Order No. 3171 relating to the Protection of Trading Interests Act, both of which penalise people and companies that comply with the extraterritorial aspects of the US blockade of Cuba. However, these laws are still not enforced decades later. British banks have closed accounts, confiscated money and refused transactions for solidarity groups and Cuban nationals, fearing the threat of US fines. Rock Around the Blockade has been blocked by PayPal, Stripe and

Facebook, and even the Cuban embassy in London has been affected. In 2017, the Open University admitted banning Cuban nationals from accessing courses, citing potential fines by the US Treasury department.

While maintaining diplomatic relations with Cuba, in the international arena, Britain has opposed the Cuban government. In 1979 Britain was one of only six countries at the UN General Assembly to vote against the 'Havana Declaration' of the Group of 77. This was a call for the industrialised countries to provide $300bn extra aid to underdeveloped economies and was proposed to the Assembly by Fidel Castro. In 1997 Britain and the European Union agreed to demands by the US to harden their stance against Cuba by condemning so-called 'human rights violations' and calling for greater democracy. In the run-up to the 1997 General Election, Tony Blair and Robin Cook, in response to letters asking them to clarify Labour's position on Cuba, condemned what they describe as Cuba's 'abuse of human rights and failure to introduce democratic elections'. Tony Blair was later elected Prime Minister of the 1997-2010 Labour government which proceeded to vote for a motion condemning Cuba at the United Nations Human Rights Commission (UNHRC), allowing it to just scrape a majority three years in a row. In 2000 Britain vetoed EU Preferential Trading Status for Cuba on the grounds of 'lack of democracy and human rights'. This was blatant hypocrisy from a Labour government that presided over the invasions of Afghanistan and Iraq and collaborated in the use of torture at secret interrogation camps in Abu Ghraib and elsewhere.

Though Britain has consistently voted against the US blockade at the United Nations, it has equally consistently supported the 1996 EU 'Common Position' on Cuba, suppressing trade and diplomatic relations between the EU and Cuba. In 2003, following an alleged crackdown on US-funded 'dissidents' in Cuba, Britain and other EU states froze contact with the Cuban government. Cuban cultural events were boycotted and embassies began inviting Cuban counter-revolutionaries to diplomatic events. By 2005 the EU had restored high-level contact with Cuba but member states, including Britain, retained contact with these counter-revolutionaries. In contrast, in 2014 Rene Gonzalez, one of the Cuban Five heroes previously imprisoned for infiltrating and foiling the terrorist plots of violent Cuban exiles in Miami, was denied a visa to visit the UK by the British government. Rene had been invited by MPs to address a meeting in parliament and was also due to speak the Trade Union Congress. The Court of Appeal ruled against the ban, citing the European Convention on Human Rights on the freedom to receive and impart information.

Prince Charles visited Cuba in 2019, becoming the first British royal to do so, whilst in 2018 newly elected Cuban President Diaz-Canal visited Britain, signalling Britain's increased interest in investment and trade with Cuba. Nevertheless, Britain refuses to stand up against US sanctions on Cuba, even in its own interests.

- 7 -
Cuba today
socialism and democracy

All states and systems of government are ruled by particular classes. Under Cuban socialism, it is the working class who rule. Their power is expressed through mass organisations, through people's militias and the armed forces and through the system of People's Power.

Before the revolution only Cubans who could read and write and those with property could vote, women were excluded until after the reforms of 1933. Multi-party elections took place in 1940, 1944 and 1948 but successive governments were pliant to US interests, dogged by corruption and failed to improve the conditions of the working class and poor. The election of 1952 was prevented by Batista, who was once again standing for elections and launched a coup when it was predicted he would lose. Cuba's experience of liberal multi-party elections had not solved its problems. It was no surprise that the 1959 revolution swept the old institutions aside and refused to replicate the bourgeois 'democracy' which had failed the majority of Cubans.

From 1974 new organs of People's Power were created and a socialist constitution was approved by popular referendum in 1976. At the height of the Special Period, in 1993, around three million workers met in special assemblies. Many of their proposals were implemented as the government sought to deal with the crisis. Such mass participation, unique to socialism, has been central to building consensus around Cuba's economic and political model throughout the revolution.

In Britain, the entire state machine – politicians, judges, police, army and bureaucrats – exists to maintain the rule of capitalism. It is little surprise that millions don't see any point in voting. British general elections have had turnout figures around 65% between 2001 and 2019. Britain's 2017 'snap' general election cost £140m with £41.6m spent on party campaigning. Donations from huge capitalist corporations, wealthy individuals and the big trade unions keep this expensive system afloat, buying their candidates in the process.

In Cuba, 80% of all those aged 14 and over are members of their local Committees for the Defence of the Revolution (CDRs), neighbourhood organisations set up in 1960 to defend communities against counter-revolutionary attacks. Committees exist in every community across Cuba and their responsibilities range from civil defence and discussing government proposals, to organising voluntary work, vaccination drives and cultural events. Almost all Cuban workers in the state sector and over 80% of non-state sector workers belong to a trade union and discuss matters relating to their workplace in monthly assemblies. The Cuban workers confederation (CTC) includes all Cuban unions and trade unionists.

The Communist Party of Cuba has more than 600,000 members and provides important political and social leadership to the Cuban people, alongside its youth wing, the Union of Young Communists (UJC). There are members in every workplace and institution, as well as in local and national government, though the Party itself does not stand in elections.

50% of those people making up the legislative and executive powers are nominated by the people at constituency level. The other half are nominated by mass organisations, including the CTC, CDR, the Women's Federation (FMC), the farmers' union (ANAP), the University Students' Federation (FEU) and the Intermediate Level Students' Federation (FEEM). Municipal elections take place every two and a half years and National Assembly elections every five. Candidates stand as individuals, rather than on the ticket of a political party. They are nominated from their municipalities and mass organisations then elected by direct, secret ballot. The only form of campaigning allowed is a photo and biography. Those elected continue in their previous employment, continue to receive their previous wage and can be recalled by referendum by their municipality. There is no room for the political careerism or exorbitant expenses allowances so prevalent in Britain. The President, Prime Minister and all those elected to government must go through two elections: first as a deputy in their constituency and then by the National Assembly. Every election held in Cuba since the revolution has had a high turnout, often above 90%.

Deciding the future of Cuban socialism

From August to November 2018, in neighbourhood centres, workplaces and schools, over 133,600 meetings took place to discuss a draft of a new constitution of the Republic of Cuba. Over 8,900,000 people took part, a massive exercise in participatory democracy. There were intense debates on wide ranging issues including same-sex marriage and diverse forms of property. In February 2019, the Cuban people voted (by 86.8% 'yes' to 9% 'no') to adopt the new constitution. Having initially been excluded from the draft proposal, the goal of building communism was reinserted in the final constitutional document due to popular demand, showing the profound class-consciousness of the Cuban people. The depth to which the whole nation was involved in debating, discussing and amending the new constitution is testimony to its authenticity, an inspiring example of popular power in practice.

- 8 -

Health care as a human right

In rich, imperialist Britain, health is dependent on wealth; diseases of poverty such as anaemia and tuberculosis are on the increase. Children from the poorest 15% of the population are twice as likely to die before the age of 15 years as children from the richest 10%. In 2018 it was reported that life expectancy has started to fall for the first time in 100 years, and infant mortality is increasing. The Labour government of 1997-2010 started a remorseless process of privatisation of health care in the interests of capitalism which continued apace under the 'ConDem' 2012 Health and Social Care Act. Through the Private Finance Initiative (PFI) hospitals have become commodities which can be traded between multinationals. As of 2019, the PFI debt totalled £55bn. The Covid-19 pandemic has exposed the extent to which the NHS has been ravaged – as well as the deep inequalities in health outcomes for the poorest, particularly those from black and minority ethnic backgrounds. Personal protective equipment stocks were severely limited and the provision of hospital beds and ventilators was far lower than what was required. There is no doubt that thousands of avoidable deaths, directly or indirectly caused by the pandemic, occurred as a result of NHS cuts.

In the nations systematically underdeveloped by imperialism, six million children under the age of five die every year from preventable disease and malnutrition. In 1989, Fidel Castro pointed out: 'It is as if a bomb similar to the ones dropped on Hiroshima and Nagasaki were dropped every three days on the poor children of the world.'

Cuba has a health care system equal to the best in the world, and health care is free at the point of delivery to all citizens. Cuba's highly developed, state biotech industry is responsible for many important advances, including the world's first effective meningitis B vaccine, various cancer treatments and the first synthetic vaccine for the prevention of pneumonia. Health care has been transformed by concentrating on preventative care and by close co-operation between health care sectors. Since the revolution triumphed in 1959, infant mortality has improved from 60 per 1,000 live births to 4 per 1,000 live births in 2018. Life expectancy has also grown from 59 years to 77 for males and 81 for females, higher than the United States. Cuba has nine doctors per one thousand residents, the third highest in the world. Cuba has not had a single reported case of measles since 1993, nor rubella since 1989, nor mumps since 2010, nor whooping cough since 1994. Health is a priority.

This infrastructure and progress was tested by the Covid-19 pandemic. In an exemplary response, Cuba's socialist health care system and community organisation enabled the entire population to be regularly screened whilst an efficient system of testing, contact tracing and quarantine centres was put into place. (see Appendix II)

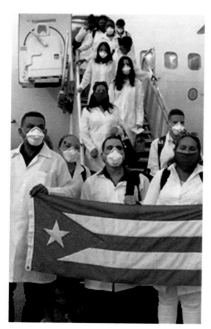

Cuba also has an outstanding record of internationalist health solidarity. For more than 60 years tens of thousands of Cuban doctors have voluntarily risked their lives to provide much needed medical care to people in desperate need across the globe, whilst the Latin American School of Medicine in Havana trains thousands of doctors from under-served communities around the globe in an outstanding feat of medical solidarity. These efforts have been redoubled during the Covid-19 pandemic (see chapter 12).

Only a nationalised health service can provide health care for the mass of the working class and such a system can only be fully developed and protected in a socialist society such as that which exists in Cuba.

9

Education for the masses

In 1958, before the revolution, there were just 82 high schools and two universities in the whole of Cuba. The revolutionary government devoted considerable resources to ensure a system of universal, free and compulsory education. Within ten years of the revolution every Cuban child had access to primary education and over 80% were enrolled in high school.

Today, enrolment in primary and secondary education is over 99% whilst in 2016 over 500,000 students were enrolled in 41 universities. Provided they pass entrance exams, every Cuban student can study to postgraduate level without charge. Cuba was recognised by the World Bank in 2014 as having the best education system in Latin America and the Caribbean. According to UNESCO data in 2015, 13% of Cuba's national budget is spent on education, one of the highest proportions of any country in the world and around twice the proportion spent by Britain. In 2019, Save The Children reported that Cuba is the safest country in Latin America and the Caribbean for children and adolescents. As billboards in Havana proclaim, 'Tonight, throughout the world, 200 million children will sleep on the streets. Not one of them is Cuban'.

Whilst in Britain, the education system is competitive and elitist with around 40 children a day permanently excluded from school; the Cuban education system emphasises the importance of an 'all-round' education, where co-operation not competition is the guiding principle. It stresses the need for academic, technical, physical, spiritual and artistic opportunities. This is seen as the key to personal development which in turn will enrich society as a whole. Cuban children are part of democratic processes in ways that are totally alien to capitalist countries. During Cuban elections, children guard the ballot boxes and count the votes. Cuban children are also organised to represent their own interests – 98% of students from the ages of 5 to 15 are in the Pioneers, a mass organisation of school students. Pupils elect a *jefe* (chief) in each classroom, who reports to

the *Colectivo,* or student council for the whole school. The *Colectivo* is made up of nine elected members, a *presidente* and eight elected jefes, each with a responsibility over: emulation, work, culture, study, sports, activities, politics, and the school. The *Colectivo* serves on the school council and is involved in the running of the school.

Students also receive vocational training via the Pioneers youth organisation and are encouraged to take part in voluntary work, such as cleaning their school, helping recycle materials from their home or working in communal gardens. The Pioneer Centres integrate facilities for play and extracurricular learning. Anything from instrumental music, medical technology and sculpture to poetry, organic gardening and boxing can become the focus of an interest group. Free public video clubs and computer centres also promote access to the internet, IT and international film whilst theatre, music concerts and ballet are heavily subsidised or free for Cubans, promoting access to culture. Although resources are often squeezed by the blockade, every municipality has the capacity to print material for all artists and writers, helping new creators get copies of their work in print.

Venezuelan author Carlos Mendez Ovary, in his 1995 book *Democracy in Cuba?* explains that in Cuba: 'These successes are not plucked out of the air. They are the result of a concern for culture that begins with considerable state funding and continues with painstaking efforts at infrastructural and organisational levels. And this is what has taken place and fulfilled the words of the Cuban constitution that define culture as an inalienable right of working people who enjoy it from childhood.'

10

Women in Cuba

the revolution within the revolution

Before the 1959 revolution, Cuban women made up 9.8% of the workforce and only 13.7% of all adult women were employed outside the home. According to the 1953 national census 87,522 women were working as low-waged domestic servants, 77,500 were working without pay for family members, and 21,000 were unemployed. Around 83% of all employed women in Cuba worked less than ten weeks each year, and only 14% worked year-round. An estimated 100,000 women were working as prostitutes; there were some 270 brothels in Havana alone. Abortion was illegal and contraception practically non-existent.

Cuba's socialist revolution ripped off the shackles imposed on women under capitalism and created the conditions for gender equality. Vilma Espin, who had been central to civilian resistance in Santiago and on the second Eastern Front during the revolutionary war, founded the Federation of Cuban Women (FMC) in 1960, empowering women to participate more fully in the revolution. Always a committed communist, Espin was the first woman in the political bureau of the Cuban Communist Party and the Council of State.

The Family Code of 1975 pioneered by Espin was important in legally mandating for equality in the domestic sphere. Today the FMC boasts four million members – more than 90% of all Cuban women over the age of 14. Speaking to *Granma* in 2016 Teresa Amarelle Boue, the Secretary General of the FMC, was clear that 'among our fundamental purposes is the defence of the revolution; because if we compare

what we were and what we are, there is no alternative.'

The FMC organise through *Casas de orientaciones* in each municipality, centres where women come for support with meetings, education, support during pregnancy, sexual health, family mediation, childcare, and age specific issues. All members are connected to other mass organisations in Cuba such as the Cuban Workers Federation (CTC) and Committees for the Defence of the Revolution (CDR). The organisation of society means these organisations work together to provide integrated specialist support – a pregnant woman can receive help from the FMC, her local family doctor, the maternity home, her workplace and her local CDR.

As of 2018 Cuban women make up 53.2% of the National Assembly – the second highest percentage of women in parliament in the world, and the highest in the Americas. By contrast, Britain was 39th on the list with women only making up 33.8% of Parliament, and the US congress ranks 109th. Eight out of 15 provinces in Cuba are led by women. Women constitute 60% of all professionals, 78.5% of health care professionals, 53% of scientists, and 66% of highly trained technicians. Cuban women represent 60% of university graduates and eight in 10 attorneys are women. Since 2018, women not only make up the majority of those in professional areas of work but they also hold two-thirds of the positions in Cuba's science and technology sector. This is one of the highest proportions in the world, compared to roughly one quarter in Europe. Women in Cuba make up 50% of those who work in engineering, while in Britain, in 2017, the figure was just 11%.

The infrastructure created by socialism has been vital in enabling women to fulfil their intellectual and social potential. The full political support of the state has been necessary for women's equality and liberation. In Cuba, this has included free access to health care and education, decent employment at equal pay and sexual and reproductive rights.

One part of this is the maternal-infant health programme which includes over 12 check-ups for pregnant people; provision of contraceptives; free, legal abortions; reduction in infant mortality rate (which is already among the lowest in the world); and check-ups every week for newborns. Cuba prioritises cervical, uterine and breast cancer screenings, has a programme to prevent sexually transmitted infections and within the support for older adults' programme offers specific initiatives for elderly women. WHO recognised Cuba as being the first country to eliminate mother-to-child HIV and syphilis. The FMC visits maternity centres across the country where they offer support and advice to

women about safe sex, as well as working within communities to support those at risk of prostitution or domestic violence, carrying out prevention efforts and offering guidance. In Britain, the women's refuge budget was slashed by £7.3 million between 2011 and 2017 with some domestic abuse services reporting an 80% funding cut and others being destroyed altogether.

Cuba offers two years of free nursery education, enabling mothers to continue to participate in political and social life. To ensure adequate financial support and security, mothers receive six months of paid breastfeeding breaks and increased and extended maternity monetary benefits – which apply to all women in the state sector as well as workers in special schemes (self-employed, artists etc). When they return to work, women can continue to claim the benefit alongside their salary until their child turns one. Paternity leave is available for two years at 60% of salary, and this has now been extended to grandparents. The FMC is leading the work on extending and improving access to childcare centres.

Nevertheless, women in Cuba still face problems, mostly lack of financial and material resources which reflect the wider situation imposed by the US blockade. There is a prevailing '*machismo*' culture – while socialism provides the framework for equality, chauvinist views persist in some individuals. However, organisations like the FMC are directly challenging this through initiatives like the *Evoluciona* campaign against sexual harassment on the street, working in schools and workplaces, displaying billboards and running clips on TV channels to raise awareness. Unlike under capitalism where the institutionalised oppression of women is systemic, the revolution is committed to battling and eliminating sexism in all its forms and continues to strive for full women's emancipation.

- 11 -
Climate emergency
Cuba leads the way

Climate change is already happening. The pollution poured into the atmosphere is fuelling runaway global warming. Just 100 companies are responsible for 71% of all emissions. Climate scientists say CO_2 emissions must be cut by at least 36bn tonnes to avoid a catastrophic 2°C temperature rise on pre-industrial times, which we are on course to hit by 2050. Despite this, global carbon emissions increased by 2.7% in 2018. This ever-increasing output is not matched by improvements in global living standards, inequality continues to soar. Capitalism cannot solve the climate crisis.

In contrast, Cuba is a world reference point for environmental sustainability, an inspiring example of an alternative society. In 2006 the World Wildlife Fund 'Living planet' report identified Cuba as the only country in the world to have achieved sustainable development, with a high level of human development (0.8 UN Human Development Index score) coupled with a low carbon footprint (ecological footprint less than 1.8 per global hectare). In 2019 new research by the Sustainable Development Index ranked Cuba as the most sustainably developed country on the planet.

The 2019 constitution includes the commitment to 'promote the conservation of the environment and the fight against climate change, which threatens the survival of the human species'. Central to this is democracy, placing energy and planning 'in the hands of the people' under the control and organisation of municipalities, made up of Committees for the Defence of the Revolution and other grassroots community organisations which promote renewable energy use and ecology house by house, block by block. The Cuban government has leapt into action. In 2019, a trial of solar powered water heaters was launched and a new fisheries law was enacted with provisions to curtail illegal fishing, preserve coral reefs, recover fish populations and protect small-scale fishers.

Cuba has long been experimenting with renewable energy and ecology. However, the drive to reduce fuel consumption and improve efficiency assumed critical importance after the collapse of the Soviet Union in 1991. Food, gas, and oil became scarce as the US attempted to suffocate Cuba by tightening the blockade. Faced with the urgent need to preserve the socialist revolution, Cuba restructured its agriculture, energy and transport along ecological, efficient lines

The National Energy Development Programme was implemented to maximise efficiency. All rural schools, health clinics, and social centres in the country, not previously connected to the grid, were electrified with solar energy. A huge reforestation programme was launched in 1998. Now 30.6% of land is covered by forest and Cuba is identified by the UN's Food and Agriculture organisation as the most advanced in reforestation in Latin America and the Caribbean. In the Special Period there was a big push to develop urban farming and reduce food miles. Organic and permaculture methods were developed as man-made fertilisers and pesticides were scarce. In Havana alone, 35,000 hectares of land are now used for *organiponico* urban farms.

In 2006 the 'Energy Revolution' sought to decrease energy wastage and loss. In a feat of popular power and community organisation, 13,000 social workers, recruited from young people who were not in education or employment, visited homes, factories and businesses, replacing incandescent light bulbs with energy saving bulbs free of charge, and offering energy saving education. In six months over nine million incandescent light bulbs were changed making Cuba the first country in the world to eliminate inefficient tungsten filament lighting.

Millions of energy efficient refrigerators, rice cookers and fans were sold at highly subsidised prices. Cuba replaced its old electrical plants with nearly 2,000 micro-electrical fuel plants, promoting decentralised power production and improving efficiency. This alone allowed Cuba to save over 961,000

tonnes of oil. The Energy Revolution increased the installed capacity of energy production by 22% whilst decreasing CO2 emissions by 5 million tonnes, an outstanding achievement.

The Energy Revolution continues today. In 2017 Cuba embarked on a drive to replace 13 million fluorescent lamps with LEDs and substitute 2 million electric resistance cookers for induction cookers alongside the installation of 250,000 LED street lighting lamps. In its 10-year 'Plan 2030' the National Assembly of People's Power aims to increase renewable energy sources to generate 24% of electricity needs by the end of the decade. In 2019, around 5% of Cuba's electricity was produced by renewable sources, as the focus had been on reducing usage and promoting efficiency. However, around 20% of primary energy production is from renewable sources due to the use of biomass.

Cuba's main biomass use is driven by the nation's sugar industry in which bagasse – pulp residue from the processing of sugar cane – is burned to produce steam for turbines that power the sugar processing plant and feed into the electrical grid. The country's first bioelectric plant in Ciego de Avila began operation in 2020, and generates over 157 kilowatts of energy for every tonne of sugar cane processed at an interconnected sugar mill. Biogas is also widely promoted, a renewable energy source produced by the fermentation of agricultural crop waste or manure. In addition to large scale biogas facilities, small farms are supported to set up small scale biodigesters using waste from cattle. There are four industrial wind farms in Cuba and as of 2017, 22 solar farms were in operation – with plans for another 50 to be built. Even rum contributes to the ecological drive; the Cubay rum distillery in Santa Cruz uses solar panels and biogas digesters to produce fertiliser and water for agriculture from the waste-water of the distillation process, producing electricity for the national grid.

Cuba only emits 0.08% of the world's greenhouse gases but it will be disproportionately affected by climate change. Preparing for this, Cuba has devised a 100-year plan to protect its population against the worst effects; *Tarea Vida* (Project Life). This includes moving low lying populations further inland, preventing new housing construction in areas prone to sea flooding, breeding strains of crops resistant to higher temperatures and promoting beach recovery and defensive reforestation. The plan focuses on disaster reduction by using the country's scientific capacity to reduce the danger, vulnerability and territorial risk. As we face the climate crisis worldwide, we have so much to learn from Cuba's approach.

- 12 -
Revolution and the fight against racism

Racism is at the heart of imperialism. The wealth of imperialist countries is founded on the super-exploitation and oppression of poor nations whilst within the imperialist nations themselves, institutional, systemic racism is used to divide the working class, forcing black people into poverty, restricting education, housing and employment opportunities, with police and fascist thugs brutalising any resistance to such discrimination. Imperialism cannot be anything other than racist.

Cuba's role as a major sugar-producing colony was founded on slavery. However, since the triumph of the revolution in 1959, Cuba has set about building a socialist society based on equality. As Assata Shakur, a former member of the US Black Panther Party, who has lived in Cuba since 1985, puts it:

'The first lesson I learned was that revolution is a process, so I was not that shocked to find sexism had not totally disappeared in Cuba, nor had racism, but that although they had not totally disappeared the revolution was totally committed to struggling against racism and sexism in all their forms... You cannot wipe out racism or sexism unless you have some kind of system that guarantees basic human rights and food and shelter and is humanistic... Cuba has the social system that will eventually wipe out racism!'
(Interview for Fight Racism! Fight Imperialism! 131 June/July 1996)

Following elections in 2018, three of the six vice presidents of the Council of State are black, including the first vice president; two are black women.

Nonetheless, black Cubans say they are more likely to be stopped by the police and less likely to find jobs in the better paid tourism sector. As those who fled Cuba in 1959 were predominantly Hispanic Cubans who had benefited from the racist Batista regime, wealthier emigres send more remittances back to their families in Cuba, which has led to material divisions between white and black Cubans. However, within Cuban society there exists the possibility

of change and the determination to carry that through. The Communist Party has made a point of promoting young black activists to prominent political positions, insisting that racism at any level will not be tolerated.

In 2015, members of the Black Lives Matter movement's Black Youth Project 100 reflected on their visit to Cuba remarking: 'many of the Black Lives Matter movement's "radical" demands to alleviate the effects of structural racism have been fulfilled in Cuba: all education is free, health care is free, housing is subsidised, healthy food is subsidised, and more. In 1962 the Cuban government declared the end of racial discrimination through the implementation of these egalitarian policies. In the US, racism is aggressive and deadly, systemic and carefully calculated. Although not fully eradicated...Cuba's socialist model diminishes the presence of structural racism and Cubans rightfully take pride in being more socially advanced than the US in their "pursuit" for racial equality.'

Cuba continues to challenge the imperialist system that lies at the heart of racism, whether by sending troops to Angola in 1975 to fight apartheid South Africa's army, sending doctors and health care workers to support impoverished communities around the globe, or challenging the unpayable burden of debt imperialism imposes on the poor countries of the world.

'Cuba is not only talking about racism in abstract terms, but connecting it with imperialism, the underlying motor of racism today... Anybody who is honestly struggling with racism must struggle against imperialism and vice-versa.'

(Assata Shakur, speaking to Pastors for Peace, Cuba, November 2000)

LGBT rights in revolutionary Cuba

'I have never been in favour, nor have I promoted, nor supported, policies against homosexuals ... [I consider] it to be one of the natural aspects and tendencies of human beings which should be respected... I am absolutely opposed to any form of repression, contempt, scorn or discrimination with regard to homosexuals.'
Fidel Castro, 1992.

Attitudes and policies in Cuba relating to LGBT people have changed for the better since the revolution. This is significant considering the fact that Cuba is in the Caribbean, where 8 of the 28 states have yet to fully legalise same-sex sexual relations, 64% have no anti-discrimination laws in place and 75% have no laws concerning gender/identity expression.

Before the revolution triumphed in 1959, the majority of Cuba's LGBT population was concentrated in Havana. At the time there was a lucrative industry of gambling, drugs and prostitution which served foreign tourists, with some travelling to Cuba seeking LGBT sex workers in particular. This trapped many LGBT people in illicit sexualised labour, relying on rich elites and US military personnel for their livelihoods. The profits from this industry meant that capitalists and organised criminals encouraged LGBT people to work in these sectors, yet this didn't translate to tolerance in wider society.

After 1959, the trend of the already existent machismo in Cuban society continued. Due to the legacy of Spanish colonialism and the orthodox Catholicism it championed, hostility to LGBT people was the norm in the region. Military Units to Aid Production (UMAP) existed in Cuba from 1965 to 1968. Gay men were amongst the people who went to UMAP as an alternative to military service, though they made up less than 10% of the camps' population. Protests by the Cuban Writers and Artists Federation against poor treatment by those in charge of the camps led to Fidel Castro performing an undercover inspection. He witnessed the abuse happening within them and ordered them to be shut down.

In 1975 the Cuban government opened a commission on homosexuality which led to its decriminalisation in 1979. When AIDS broke out in 1981, Cuba began to tirelessly work for a cure. As early as 1983, Cuba established the National Commission for the control of AIDS and drew up a programme for all hospitals. As in other parts of the world, the condition was initially viewed as a 'gay disease', however this changed in 1988 when a study revealed that gay or bisexual men only accounted for 25% of cases, while heterosexual men accounted for 50%. This resulted in a change of Cuban attitudes towards sexual diversity, as discrimination was now recognised as harmful both to those being discriminated against and those engaged in discrimination. Today the Caribbean is the world's second-most affected region in terms of HIV prevalence rates, yet Cuba holds one of the lowest rates in the world, at 0.4%.

Throughout the 1980s state bodies ran courses on sexual health at FMC meetings, community centres and schools, discussing sexual diversity and promoting education to counter homophobia. In the 1990s the Ministry of Culture supported films, plays and music with openly LGBT themes, a cultural push that continues today.

The National Centre for Sex Education (CENESEX), was founded in 1989 and is headed by Mariela Castro, daughter of Raul Castro and Vilma Espin, founder of the Cuban Women's Federation. This government body has become a focal point for LGBT politics and rights in Cuba with much of its work focused on the rights of transgender people. Gender reassignment surgery has been paid for by the state since 2008, accompanied by a holistic approach to mental health and social support. Education in communities is key and is evidently having an impact; In 2012 Adela Hernandez, a trans woman, was elected into the municipal council of Caibarien in Villa Clara.

Lucy, who took part in a Rock around the Blockade brigade to Cuba in 2019, wrote on her return: 'As a trans-woman, navigating the NHS for the last four years, I was keen to compare my experiences. If you are trans in Britain, you either need a lot of money, or a lot of patience. The approach at CENESEX is radically different. If you are trans, you talk to your family doctor, or visit a polyclinic. There is virtually no waiting time for referrals and mental health support is provided not just for the person transitioning, but for family members also.'

The new constitution removed the section which defined marriage as between a man and a woman. This move opens the door to debate and redefine the family form in Cuba, something CENESEX is determined to do in order to improve the lives of LGBT people and families.

- 12 -
Cuban internationalism

The Cubans have always understood their revolution to be one part of the international struggle against imperialism and wherever possible have given their support to other oppressed people. The first Declaration of Havana on 2 September 1960 proclaimed, 'the duty of each nation to make common cause with all the oppressed, colonised, exploited peoples, regardless of their location in the world'. The second Declaration in 1962 asserted 'the duty of every revolutionary is to make revolution'. Cuba's stand at that time inspired guerrilla movements in Venezuela, Guatemala and Colombia.

In September 1960, when Fidel Castro first visited the United Nations in New York, the Cuban delegation chose to stay not in the luxury hotel which they had been allocated, but in Harlem where they were greeted enthusiastically by thousands of poor black people and where Fidel met with Malcolm X.

Throughout the 1960s Cuba supported national liberation movements throughout Africa. Later, it also helped with military programmes in Syria, South Yemen, Algeria, Sierra Leone and Tanzania, and gave military assistance to progressive movements in El Salvador and Nicaragua. Cuba supported SWAPO, the national liberation movement in Namibia, and the M19 guerrillas in Colombia. In 1978 Cuban troops supported Ethiopia against imperialist-inspired aggression by Somalia. From 1975 Cuba sent troops and technicians to support the MPLA government in Angola, which was under attack when apartheid South Africa's army invaded the country, supported by the US government. Some 450,000 Cuban volunteers went to Angola. The Cuban troops, fighting alongside the MPLA army, forced the South Africans back over 400 kilometres, liberating a million square kilometres of the country. In 1988 South African forces were again defeated by the Cuban and MPLA forces at the second battle of Cuito Cuanavale. This great victory decisively ended US imperialist hopes of military domination throughout southern Africa and was a huge step towards the ending of apartheid.

Cuba sent hundreds of thousands of volunteers to help build schools, hospitals and roads in Peru, Jamaica and North Vietnam. In 1979, when the Cuban government asked for 2,000 teachers, doctors and advisers to help the progressive Sandinista government in Nicaragua, 29,000 Cubans volunteered. When US forces invaded Grenada in 1983, Cuban volunteers working there joined the resistance until ordered to lay down their arms in the face of the overwhelming odds.

Since the 1970s Cuba has provided free education to tens of thousands of students from Africa and Central America to help promote development and independence from imperialist exploitation. In the United Nations, at international conferences, in world and regional forums, at every opportunity, the Cubans speak out in support of the oppressed majority of the world's people. The Cubans contrast the claims of 'western democracy' and human rights with the reality of a world where 9 million die each year from malnutrition and 780 million lack access to clean drinking water. They counter the 'neo-liberal' propaganda of the imperialist nations and their accomplices in the IMF and WTO who seek to re-colonise the oppressed nations and increase further the poverty and suffering of the people. They support those fighting back against imperialist aggression. They have repeatedly condemned the bombing of the Middle East and North Africa by US and British forces, and opposed the coups and resurgence of US-backed right wing governments in Latin America. They demonstrate their solidarity and support for the Palestinian people, call for a free Palestine and condemn the Zionist aggressors and their US imperialist backers.

Above all, the Cubans call on nations plundered by imperialism to stand together to protect their own interests. As long ago as 1979, Fidel Castro was calling for the cancellation of the so-called Third World debt. In his speech on behalf of the 107 members of the Non-Aligned Movement he said, 'Unequal exchange is ruining our peoples. It must end. ... The international monetary system is bankrupt. It must be replaced. The debts of the least developed countries ...must be cancelled. Indebtedness oppresses the rest of the developing countries ...There must be relief. The economic chasm between the developed countries and the countries seeking development is not narrowing but widening. It must be closed!' The vicious cycle of debt and extraction sees countries forced to sell their natural resources cheaply in order to service their debts, perpetuating dependency and ecological destruction.

In the 2000s, progressive, social democratic governments swept to power in many Latin American countries in a backlash against neo-liberalism and

US interference. In 2004, Fidel Castro and Venezuela's socialist President Hugo Chavez founded the Bolivarian Alliance for the Peoples of Our America (ALBA), soon joined by 10 other nations across Latin America and the Caribbean. Regional integration projects provided mutual assistance and funding for development projects, whilst millions benefited from health care and education initiatives such as Operation Miracle, which has removed cataracts and restored sight for six million people across Latin America and the Caribbean free of charge. The alliance rallied against imperialism and aimed to reduced the dependence of member countries on unilateral trade with the US. This posed a threat to US interests and ALBA quickly became a target of US aggression. US backed coups in Honduras and Bolivia and Moreno's right wing government in Ecuador pulled these nations out of the alliance, weakening the project. Though Bolivian President Arce, elected in 2020 as the Movement Towards Socialism rewgained power restablished ties with ALBA countries, the US has ramped up sanctions against remaining central members Nicaragua, Venezuela and Cuba. Nevertheless at its height, ALBA illustrated that trade and development could be based on cooperation and solidarity, placing people before profit.

Actions speak louder than words – internationalism in health care!

Alongside their call for unity and resistance, the Cubans have initiated programmes of assistance and solidarity with other poor countries. Since 1960, 400,000 Cuban medical professionals have worked overseas in 164 countries. Cuba first sent an emergency medical brigade to Chile following an earthquake in 1960. Ever since Cuban brigades have provided immediate medical relief, often free of charge, to countries desperate for support following earthquakes, tsunamis, cyclones and epidemics. Cuba sent the largest delegation of health care workers to tackle Ebola in west Africa in 2014, and in 2020 in response to the Covid-19 pandemic, Cuba sent 2,300 health care specialists to 24 countries to treat Covid patients, earning the nation's Henry Reeve International Medical Brigades a nomination for the 2020 Nobel Peace Prize. In the mid 2000s, Cuba and Venezuela signed an 'oil for doctors' programme under which 30,000 Cuban health care workers helped create a free community health programme across Venezuela. Subsequently, Cuba signed agreements for longer-term collaborations with other nations, supporting the development of health care in underserved communities whilst generating important revenue for the Cuban economy.

Cuba is also training doctors for the world. Created in 1999, the Latin American School of Medicine trains thousands from impoverished communities, free of charge. By 2019, 29,000 doctors from 105 countries had graduated, half of them young women. These projects are remarkable in their optimism and daring. They put to shame the inaction of the imperialist nations and demonstrate what could be done, even with limited resources, if the world were guided by socialist principles.

US imperialism has attacked Cuba's internationalist health projects. In 2006 US President Bush attempted to sabotage Cuba's medical export earnings by setting up the Medical Parole Programme offering US citizenship for any Cuban abandoning their overseas missions. In 2019, the Trump administration renewed attacks on Cuban medical internationalism labelling Cuban health care professionals 'slaves'. Right-wing governments in Brazil, Ecuador and Bolivia subsequently expelled Cuban medical teams, leaving millions of people in those countries without health care and cutting off an important source of income for Cuba. The reality is that Cuba's disaster response brigades are sent to impoverished nations, often without charge; whilst doctors volunteering in longer term collaborations continue to receive their Cuban salaries, plus a sizeable stipend. Cuba's health internationalism is the target of a campaign of lies and distortion precisely because it represents the threat of a good example.

- 13 -
Fighting the media war on socialism in Latin America

Progressive people and revolutionary movements around the world carry the image of Che Guevara on protests, and nations strangled by imperialism reference the internationalist support they have received from socialist Cuba, but you won't read or hear their stories in the so-called 'liberal left' *Guardian*, nor from the supposedly impartial BBC. Any faint praise for Cuba's achievements in human development, international health assistance or environmental sustainability is always accompanied by obligatory slurs and distortions about human rights, freedom of speech and democracy. No matter that narrow bourgeois definitions of human rights and democracy never stretch to the basic rights of housing, health care, education, food and culture guaranteed in Cuba, and discount the island's impressive system of participatory grassroots democracy.

Instead, mainstream media trot out false diatribes, deciding the facts that are fit to be published, and the facts that should be ignored or downplayed. These publications play a particular role in the ideological protection of corporate interests. Six multi-billion-dollar corporations control the US press and airwaves. In Britain, just three corporations, *News UK (Murdoch)*, *DMGT* and *Trinity Mirror*, control 70% of newspaper circulation. These publications lead an ideological attack on nations attempting to oppose US, European and British imperialism. Their shallow articles fail to examine the powerful financial and political interests backing opposition forces in Cuba, Venezuela and Nicaragua, fail to connect these to the US agenda for reaction in Latin America and fail to explain the renewed attempt to impose devastating IMF and World Bank austerity packages and structural adjustment programmes.

These media outlets rely on soundbites from NGOs like Amnesty International, which writes damning reports about often fabricated human rights allegations while glossing over the economic sanctions and political interference responsible for restricting food and denying medicine to the very populations they are supposed to care about. Far from being neutral, Amnesty International is well funded for toeing the line. General secretaries take home £200,000 a year and senior directors £100,000. In 2008, Britain's Department for International Development donated over £3m to Amnesty.

Cuba and the anti-imperialist movements for socialism across Latin America have long been targeted by this media war. These organisations will stop at nothing to discredit anything that smacks of socialism – deliberately obscuring the chaos and bloodshed that US intervention entails. Instead they provide a forum for reaction: a platform for powerful, right-wing Cuban exiles and their allies to spout their ideological lies and distortions.

All media has a political agenda and reporting is tailored to meet that agenda. Those which give the illusion of bourgeois democracy and critical thinking, such as *The Guardian* and BBC, have taken outrageous positions on the attacks on movements for socialism in the region, most recently backing opposition attacks to undermine the Bolivarian Revolution in Venezuela, justifying the coup against Morales in Bolivia, maintaining near-silence on political violence in Colombia and brutal police repression of protestors in Chile. Their coverage intentionally demonises the anti-imperialist struggle in Latin America, undermining the international solidarity so desperately needed. Despicably, organisations of the British left such as the Socialist Workers Party, repeat these lies and manipulations, refusing to support the socialist and progressive governments attempting to build new societies in the shadow of the strongest imperialist nation in history. Not only does this weaken the international socialist struggle but young would-be revolutionaries are turned away from the example of Cuban socialism and the inspiration it provides for anti-capitalist struggle everywhere.

The ruling class need to crush any revolutionary alternative to crisis ridden capitalism. In this task of imperialism, the role of the international press is a central weapon. As the renewed ideological onslaught gathers pace, we must expose the barefaced lies and distortions that the human rights industry and media war spew into our newsfeeds.

Rock around the Blockade

30 years of solidarity with Cuba

'Many people coming here in solidarity with Cuba ask, "what can we do: what can we send you?" However, I am convinced that the best form of solidarity that you can give to Cuba and Venezuela is *political* support. How can we break the media lies? How can we mobilise against the blockade?' Belkys Lay Rodriguez – Functionary of the Central Committee of the Communist *Party of Cuba, speaking to an RATB solidarity brigade in 2019.*

Rock around the Blockade (RATB) was set up by the Revolutionary Communist Group (RCG) in 1995 to support socialist Cuba. Active solidarity with Cuba has distinguished the RCG from the majority of the British left, enabling us to raise socialism as a viable alternative to capitalism and imperialism and move beyond idealistic sloganeering, to introduce real questions of relations of production, power and democracy. After ten years of austerity and with further savage cuts to benefits and public services on the way, the need to present a socialist alternative is greater than ever.

Our first brigade travelled to Cuba with over 30 brigadistas in December 1995 in the midst of Cuba's Special Period. The impact of the economic crisis was obvious during the brigade; conditions for Cubans were tough. We stayed in a large agricultural camp in the central province of Ciego de Avila, alongside 300 young Cubans who had volunteered to labour on the land, determined that their revolution would survive the crisis. This experience was central to our understanding of how and why the revolution retained the commitment of the majority of Cuba's population.

Since 1995, RATB has:

1. Organised 13 further solidarity brigades through Cuba's Union of Young Communists (UJC), taking over music, sport, arts and other equipment to physically break the blockade.

2. Organised three national speaking tours of Cubans in Britain: in 2002 (with Kenia Serrano and Nancy Aguiar, leading members of the UJC) in 2008 (which included Orlando Borrego, former deputy to Che Guevara in Cuban industry) and in 2019 (with Reinaldo Funes Monzote, a Cuban environmental historian).

3. Produced a documentary, Cuba: defending socialism, resisting imperialism, and many short clips and interviews, available on our YouTube channel: 'Cuba Vive'.

4. Created our website (ratb.org.uk) carrying news from Cuba and Latin America.

5. Developed educational work to break the information blockade of Cuba and gain a deeper understanding of Cuban socialism in a post-Soviet world. This pamphlet, now in its third edition, is a contribution to this work.

6. Campaigned for the freedom of the Cuban Five – arrested in 1998 and charged with spying to conspiracy to commit murder and endangering the security of the United States. These men had been working to foil the persistent attempts by right-wing counter-revolutionary groups incubated in the US to commit acts of sabotage and terrorism against Socialist Cuba. Their case illustrated the hypocrisy of the US's 'War on Terror'. Amidst international pressure the final three members were released in 2016 as a

direct result of talks between former US President Obama's administration and Cuba.

7. Campaigned to Boycott Bacardi, exposing their anti-Cuban activity. Despite already moving key aspects of their production to Spain, Mexico and Puerto Rico from as early as 1910, and being offered compensation by the revolution in 1960, Bacardi claim their assets were 'illegally confiscated without compensation'. Pepin Bosch, head of Bacardi in 1959 was linked to the CIA and Cuban exile groups attacking the emerging revolution and Bacardi continues to promote the US blockade. Exposing this we carried out Bacardi bar busts, street theatre, subvertising and appealed for conscientious drinkers to choose Havana Club, real Cuban rum, whose profits are invested back into Cuban society.

8. Picketed media companies that broadcast propaganda against Cuba and its allies. Working in collaboration with members of the Latin American community and other solidarity campaigns, RATB has targeted *The Guardian* and the BBC with protests for their hostile coverage of Cuba and Venezuela.

Picket Esso - Oppose Helms-Burton Title III!

In 2019 Rock around the Blockade and the Revolutionary Communist Group launched pickets of Esso garages in protest against ExxonMobil's lawsuit against Cuban state companies Corporation Climex SA and Union Cuba-Petroleo. The billion dollar oil multinational is hoping to claim $280m in compensation for Cuba's nationalisation of Standard Oil's Havana refinery 60 years ago. Our pickets have drawn the links between the struggle against imperialism and the fight against climate change. Some 20 lawsuits had been filed under Title III as of January 2020. We will continue to publicly target companies and individuals in Britain that attempt to capitalise on Title III of the Helms-Burton Act.

Cuba continues to build and defend socialism, providing a concrete alternative to the brutality of capitalism, imperialist war and austerity. As the US tightens the blockade and ramps up hostilities against Cuba and its allies, we must continue to oppose the illegal US blockade, to demand the end of the illegal US occupation of Guantanamo Bay and support Cuba's right to self-determination.

The main task of RATB is to bring the lessons of Cuba's revolution to working class struggles in Britain and help to build a revolutionary socialist movement. In Britain, millions of working class people live in poverty, many struggling to afford the basic necessities of life, forced into low-paid insecure jobs or facing the dehumanising benefits regime. The working class is consigned to second rate health care and education. The British government invades, bombs and exploits already impoverished countries. Police harass and attack black and Asian people and the Home Office imposes ever more punitive racist immigration laws.

In Cuba, no-one is forced to sleep on the streets, no-one starves, everyone has access to health care, education and a sense of security. No-one is abandoned, everyone has the opportunity to live with dignity. This is why it is so important that Cuba's revolution is known and understood. We all have a role to play here in Britain, to show that another world is not only possible and urgently necessary, but is being built in socialist Cuba.

IF YOU WANT TO GET INVOLVED, IF YOU WANT TO DEFEND SOCIALIST CUBA AND BUILD A NEW SOCIALIST MOVEMENT IN BRITAIN, THEN JOIN US!

Website: www.ratb.org.uk
Email: office@ratb.org.uk
Phone: 0207 837 1688
Post: BCM Box 5909, London WC1N 3XX

SOCIAL MEDIA:
Facebook:@ratbcuba
Twitter:@ratbcuba
youtube.com/ratbcuba

Tomorrow will be too late

Fidel Castro's speech to Earth Summit,
Rio de Janeiro 1992

An important biological species — humankind — is at risk of disappearing due to the rapid and progressive elimination of its natural habitat. We are becoming aware of this problem when it is almost too late to prevent it. It must be said that consumer societies are chiefly responsible for this appalling environmental destruction.

They were spawned by the former colonial metropolis. They are the offspring of imperial policies which, in turn, brought forth the backwardness and poverty that have become the scourge for the great majority of humankind.

With only 20% of the world's population, they consume two-thirds of all metals and three-fourths of the energy produced worldwide. They have poisoned the seas and the rivers. They have polluted the air. They have weakened and perforated the ozone layer. They have saturated the atmosphere with gases, altering climatic conditions with the catastrophic effects we are already beginning to suffer.

The forests are disappearing. The deserts are expanding. Billions of tons of fertile soil are washed every year into the sea. Numerous species are becoming

extinct. Population pressures and poverty lead to desperate efforts to survive, even at the expense of nature. Third World countries, yesterday's colonies and today nations exploited and plundered by an unjust international economic order, cannot be blamed for all this.

The solution cannot be to prevent the development of those who need it the most. Because today, everything that contributes to underdevelopment and poverty is a flagrant rape of the environment.

As a result, tens of millions of men, women and children die every year in the Third World, more than in each of the two world wars.

Unequal trade, protectionism and the foreign debt assault the ecological balance and promote the destruction of the environment. If we want to save humanity from this self-destruction, wealth and available technologies must be distributed better throughout the planet. Less luxury and less waste in a few countries would mean less poverty and hunger in much of the world.

Stop transferring to the Third World lifestyles and consumer habits that ruin the environment. Make human life more rational. Adopt a just international economic order. Use science to achieve sustainable development without pollution. Pay the ecological debt. Eradicate hunger and not humanity.

Now that the supposed threat of communism has disappeared and there is no more pretext to wage cold wars or continue the arms race and military spending, what then is preventing these resources from going immediately to promote Third World development and fight the ecological destruction threatening the planet?

Enough of selfishness. Enough of schemes of domination. Enough of insensitivity, irresponsibility and deceit.

Tomorrow will be too late to do what we should have done a long time ago.

Appendix II
Leading by example
Socialist Cuba in the covid-19 pandemic

The response of socialist Cuba to the global SARS-CoV2 pandemic has been outstanding both domestically and for its international contribution. That a small island nation, subjected to hundreds of years of colonialism and imperialism and, since the revolution of 1959, six decades of the criminal United States blockade, can play such an exemplary role is due to Cuba's socialist system. The central plan directs national resources according to a development strategy which prioritises human welfare and community participation, not private profit. HELEN YAFFE reports.

Cuban authorities reacted quickly to Chinese information about SARS-CoV2 at the start of the year. In January, authorities established a National Intersectoral Commission for Covid-19, updated their National Action Plan for Epidemics, initiated surveillance at ports, airports and marines, gave Covid-19 response training for border and immigration officials and drafted a 'prevention and control' plan. Cuban specialists travelled to China to learn about the new coronavirus' behaviour and commissions of the government's Scientific Council began to work on combating the coronavirus. Throughout February, medical facilities were reorganised, and staff trained to control the spread of the virus domestically. In early March a science and biotechnology group was created to develop Covid-19 treatments, tests, vaccines, diagnostics and other innovations. From 10 March inbound travellers were tested for Covid-19. All of this was before the virus was detected on the island.

On 11 March, three Italian tourists were confirmed as the first cases of Covid-19 in Cuba. Cuban health care authorities stepped into action, organising neighbourhood meetings, conducting door-to-door health checks, testing, contact tracing and quarantining. This has been accompanied by education programmes and daily information updates. The population went under 'lockdown' on 20 March, required to abide by social distancing rules and wear facemasks when leaving homes on essential business. Business taxes and domestic debts were suspended, those hospitalised had 50% of their salaries guaranteed and low-income households qualified for social assistance and family assistance schemes, with food, medicine and other goods delivered to their homes. Workshops nationwide began to produce masks, bolstered by a grassroots movement of home production, and community mutual aid groups organised to assist the vulnerable and elderly with shopping for food as long queues became the norm. On 24 March, Cuba closed its borders to all non-residents, a tough decision given the importance of tourism revenue to the state. Anyone entering the country was required to spend a fortnight in supervised quarantine, under a testing regime. Civil Defence Councils in every province and municipality were activated.

In April payment of utility bills was suspended, likewise local and regional transport, while transport was guaranteed for medical staff and other essential workers. Havana and other cities were disinfected. Twenty communities in six provinces were placed under total or partial quarantine. A Cuban-designed mobile phone app, 'Virtual Screening', went live with an opt-in application allowing users to submit an epidemiological survey for statistical analysis by the Ministry of Public Health (MINSAP). Measures were taken to keep the virus out of prisons, with active screening twice daily and no reported cases by 23 April.

By 24 May, a Cuban population of 11.2 million had reported 82 deaths and fewer than 2,000 confirmed cases; 173 confirmed cases per million people, compared to 3,907 per million in Britain. Not one health care worker had died, although 92 had been infected by mid-April.

Cuba's exemplary response is based on five features of its socialist development. First, its single, universal, free public health care system which seeks prevention over cure, with a network of family doctors responsible for community health who live among their patients. Second, Cuba's biopharma industry, which is driven by public health needs, produces nearly 70% of the medicines consumed domestically and exports to 50 countries. Third, the island's experience in civil defence and disaster risk reduction, usually in response to climate-related and natural disasters. Its internationally applauded capacity to mobilise national resources to protect human life is achieved by a network of grassroots organisations which facilitate communication and community action. Fourth, the island's experience with infectious disease (border) controls. For decades, Cuba has sent health care professionals to countries which have infectious diseases long-since eradicated on the island and has invited tens of thousands of foreigners from those countries to study in Cuba. It has well-developed procedures for quarantining people (re)entering the island. Fifth, Cuban medical internationalism, which has seen 400,000 health care professionals providing free health care for underserved populations in 164 countries; some 28,000 medical personnel were serving in 59 countries when the pandemic began. By late May, an additional 2,300 health care specialists from Cuba's Henry Reeve medical brigades, specialists in epidemiological and disaster response, had gone to 24 countries to treat patients with Covid-19.

A commitment to high-standard public health care

In 1959, Cuba had some 6,000 doctors but half of them soon left; only 12 of the 250 Cuban teachers at the University of Havana's Medical School stayed. There was only one rural hospital. The revolutionary government faced the challenge of providing a high-standard public health care system almost from scratch. To that end, in 1960, the Rural Medical Service (RMS) was established and over the next decade hundreds of newly graduated doctors were posted in remote areas. RMS physicians served as health educators as well as clinicians. National programmes were established for infectious disease control and prevention. From 1962 a national immunisation programme provided all Cubans with eight vaccinations free of charge. Infectious diseases were rapidly reduced, then eliminated. By 1970, the number of rural hospitals had reached 53. Not until 1976 was the pre-revolutionary ratio of doctors to citizens restored. By then, health services were available nationwide and indicators had improved significantly. A new model of community-based polyclinics was established in 1974 giving Cuban communities local access to primary care specialists. Training and policy emphasised the impact of biological, social, cultural, economic and environmental factors on patients. National programmes focused on maternal and child health, infectious diseases, chronic non-communicable diseases, and older adult health.

In 1983, the Family Doctor and Nurse Plan was introduced nationwide. Under this system, family doctor practices were set up in neighbourhoods, with either the doctor or the nurse living with their family above the practice, so medical attention is available 24 hours a day. Family doctors coordinate medical care and lead health promotion efforts, emphasising prevention and epidemiological analysis. They rely on history-taking and clinical skills, reserving costly high-tech procedures for patients requiring them, holding patient appointments in the mornings and making house calls in the afternoons. The teams carry out neighbourhood health diagnosis, melding clinical medicine with public health, and individualised 'Continuous Assessment and Risk Evaluation' (CARE) for their patients. Family doctors and nurses are also employed in large workplaces and schools, child day-care centres, homes for senior citizens and so on.

By 2005, Cubans had one doctor for every 167 people, the highest ratio in the world. Cuba now has 449 policlinics, each attending to 20,000 to 40,000 people and serving as a hub for 15 to 40 family doctors. There are more than 10,000 family doctors spread evenly throughout the island.

Primary Health Care as the backbone of Cuba's response

An article in April 2020 *Medicc Review* describes Cuba's primary health care system as a 'powerful weapon' against Covid-19. 'Without early access to rapid tests, massive testing was clearly not on the cards as a first strategic option. However, primary health care was.' Cuban authorities ensured that everyone in the health care system, including support staff, received Covid-19 training before the virus was detected. Senior medics from each province were trained at Cuba's world-famous hospital for tropical diseases, Instituto Pedro Kourí. On returning to their provinces they then trained colleagues in the second tier – hospital and polyclinics directors. 'Then they went on to the third tier: training for family doctors and nurses themselves, lab and radiology technicians, administrative personnel, and also housekeeping staff, ambulance drivers and orderlies. Anyone who might come into contact with a patient', explained a polyclinic director, Dr Mayra Garcia, cited in the *Medicc* article.

Each polyclinic also trained non-health sector people in their geographical area, in workplaces, small business owners, people renting homes, especially to foreigners, or managing childcare facilities, telling them how to recognise symptoms and take protective measures. Senior medical professionals in the polyclinics were sent to family doctors' offices as reinforcement. Medical staff were posted in local hotels to provide 24-hour detection and health care to foreigners residing there. Walk-in emergency services were re-organised to separate anyone with respiratory symptoms and to provide 24-hour assessment. Non-Covid-19 related appointments were postponed where possible, or shifted to home visits for priority groups.

The *Medicc* article underscores the importance of the CARE model for combating Covid-19. All Cubans are already categorised into four groups:

apparently healthy, with risk factors for disease, ill, and in recovery or rehabilitation. Doctors know the health characteristics and needs of the community they serve. 'The CARE model also automatically alerts us to people who are more susceptible to respiratory infections, the people whose chronic diseases are the risk factors most commonly associated with complications in Covid-19 patients' explained Dr Alejandro Fadragas.

Throughout Cuba, CDRs, or street committees, organised public health information meetings for family doctors and nurses to advise neighbourhoods about the pandemic. Once the first cases were confirmed, the family doctors daily house visits were extended and became the 'single most important tool' for active case detection, to get ahead of the virus. Some 28,000 medical students joined them going door to door to detect symptoms. This procedure means the whole population can be surveyed.

People with symptoms are remitted to their local polyclinic for rapid evaluation. Those suspected of having Covid-19 are sent on to one of the new municipal isolation centres established throughout the island. They must remain for a minimum of 14 days, receiving testing and medical attention. If the case appears to be another respiratory illness, they return home but must stay indoors for at least 14 days, followed up in primary care. Hospitals are reserved for patients who really need them.

Primary health care professionals are also responsible for rapid contact tracing for all suspected cases; those contacts are tested and must isolate at home. In addition, the homes and communal entrances of patients sent to isolation centres are disinfected by 'rapid response' teams consisting of polyclinic directors and vice directors, alongside family members. Family doctors' offices are also disinfected daily. Meanwhile, workers in hotels where foreigners are lodged are checked daily by medical staff. The polyclinic provides them with PPE and disinfectants. Polyclinics and family doctors are also responsible for 14 days follow-up for Covid-19 patients discharged from hospitals.

Home-grown medicine

The Cuban treatment protocol for Covid-19 patients includes 22 drugs, most produced domestically. The focus has been placed on prevention, with measures to improve innate immunity. Early on the potential of Cuba's anti-viral drug Heberon, an interferon Alfa 2b human recombinant, was identified. The biotech product has proven effective for viral diseases including hepatitis types B and C, shingles, HIV-AIDS, and dengue. Produced in Cuba since 1986 and in China since 2003 through a Cuban-Chinese joint venture, ChangHeber, in January 2020 it was selected by the Chinese National Health Commission among 30 treatments for Covid-19 patients. It soon topped their list of anti-viral drugs, having demonstrated good results.

The drug has most efficacy when used preventatively and at early stages of infection. In Wuhan, China, nearly 3,000 medical personnel received Heberon as a preventative measure to boost their immune response; none of them contracted the virus. Meanwhile, 50% of another 3,300 medics who were not given the drug did get Covid-19. Interferon Alfa 2b is recommended in the medical protocols of several countries, by the World Health Organisation (WHO), Johns Hopkins Medical Centre and the *World Journal of Paediatrics* among others. The product was already registered in Algeria, Argentina, Chile, Ecuador, Jamaica, Thailand, Venezuela, Vietnam, Yemen and Uruguay. By mid-April requests for its use had been received from some 80 countries and it was being administered by Cuba's Henry Reeve medical brigades treating Covid-19 patients overseas. On 14 April it was reported that 93.4% of Covid-19 patients in Cuba had been treated with Heberon and only 5.5% of those had reached a serious state. The mortality rate reported by that date was 2.7% but for patients treated with Heberon it was just 0.9%.

Other Cuban medicines reporting promising results include:
- Biomodulina T, an immunomodulator which stimulates the immune systems of vulnerable individuals and has been used in Cuba for 12 years, principally to treat recurrent respiratory infections in the elderly.
- The monoclonal antibody Itolizumab (Anti-CD6), used to treat lymphomas and leukemia, administered to Covid-19 patients in a severe or critical condition to reduce the secretion of inflammatory cytokines, which cause the massive flow of substances and liquid in the lungs.
- CIGB-258, a new immunomodulatory peptide designed to reduce inflammatory processes. By 22 May, 52 Covid-19 patients had been treated with CIGB-258; among those in a severe stage, the survival rate was 92%. For those in a critical condition the survival rate was 78%.

Blood plasma from recovered patients

Cuban medical scientists are producing their own version of Kaletra, an antiretroviral combination of Lopinavir and Ritonavir, used to treat HIV/AIDS. Domestic production will eliminate costly imports from capitalist big pharma and subject to the US blockade. Meanwhile, the homeopathic medicine Prevengho-Vir, which is believed to strengthen the immune system has been distributed for free to everyone on the island. Medical scientists are evaluating two vaccines to stimulate the immune system and four candidates for specific preventative vaccine for Covid-19 are under design.

By early May, Cuban scientists had adapted SUMA, a Cuban computerised diagnostic system, to detect antibodies for Covid-19 rapidly, allowing for mass testing at low cost. 'The objective is to find new cases and then intervene, isolate, seek contacts, and take all possible measures to ensure that Cuba continues as it is now', said Cuba's top epidemiologist, Francisco Durán during his daily televised update on 11 May. This means the island no longer relies on donated tests or expensive ones purchased internationally. Cuba's comparatively high rate of testing is set to soar.

BioCubaFarma is mass producing facemasks, personal protective equipment (PPE) and medical and sanitary products, as well as coordinating state enterprises and self-employed workers to repair vital equipment, such as breathing ventilators. Cuban efforts to purchase new ventilators have been obstructed by the US blockade which, for almost 60 years, has included food and medicines among its prohibitions.

Leading the global fight

On 18 March, Cuba allowed the cruise ship MS Braemar, with 684 mostly British passengers and five confirmed Covid-19 cases, to dock in Havana after a week stranded at sea, having been refused entry by Curacao, Barbados, Bahamas, Dominican Republic and the United States. Cuban authorities facilitated their safe transfer to charter flights for repatriation. Three days later, a 53-strong Cuban medical brigade arrived in Lombardy, Italy, at that time the epicentre of the pandemic, to assist local health care authorities. The medics were members of Cuba's Henry Reeve Contingent, which received a WHO Public Health Prize in 2017 in recognition for providing free emergency medical aid. It was the first Cuban medical mission to Europe. By 21 May, over 2,300 Cuban health care professionals had gone to 24 countries to treat Covid-19 patients, including a second brigade in northern Italy and another to the European principality Andorra.

The threat of a good example

Cuban medical internationalism began in 1960, but the export of health care professionals was not a source of state revenue until the mid-2000s with the famous 'oil for doctors' programme under which 30,000 Cuban health care workers served in Venezuela. US President Bush's administration responded by attempting to sabotage Cuba's medical export earnings with the Cuban Medical Parole Programme. This induced Cuban professionals, who had paid no tuition costs, graduated debt free and voluntarily signed contracts to work abroad assisting underserved populations, to abandon missions in return for US citizenship. President Obama kept the Programme, even while praising Cuban medics combating Ebola in West Africa. It was ended in his last days in office in January 2017.

The Trump administration has renewed attacks on Cuban medical missions, fuelling their expulsion from Brazil, Ecuador and Bolivia, and leaving millions of people in those countries without health care. The motivation was the same; to block revenues to a nation which has survived 60 years of US hostility. In the context of the pandemic, when the US government's wilful failures have resulted in tens of thousands of unnecessary deaths, socialist Cuba's global leadership has represented the threat of a good example. Lashing out, the US State Department has labelled Cuban medics 'slaves', claiming that the Cuban government seeks revenues and political influence. It has pressured beneficiary countries to reject Cuban assistance in their time of urgent need. These attacks are particularly vile; it is likely that Cuba is receiving no payment, beyond costs, for this assistance.

Meanwhile, the criminal US blockade, which has been punitively tightened under Trump, is preventing the purchase of urgently needed ventilators for Cuba's own Covid-19 patients. A Chinese donation to Cuba of medical equipment was blocked because the airline carrying the goods would not travel to Cuba for fear of US fines. There is now a growing international demand for an end to all sanctions, not least against Cuba which has shown global leadership in combating the pandemic. We must all add our voices to this demand. There are also calls from organisations worldwide to nominate Cuba's Henry Reeve Contingents for a Nobel Peace Prize. What is clear from its history of principled medical internationalism is that, with recognition or without, revolutionary Cuba will continue to fight for global health care wherever its citizens, and its example, can reach.

Published in FIGHT RACISM! FIGHT IMPERIALISM! 276 June/July 2020

Further Reading

For an indepth understanding of the economic ideas of Che Guevara
Che Guevara: The Economics of Revolution, Helen Yaffe (Palgrave Macmillan 2009)

For a deeper understanding of Cuba from the special period into the 21st Century
We are Cuba! How a revolutionary people have survived in a post-Soviet world, Helen Yaffe, (Yale 2020)

Both books available to order on our website:
www.revolutionarycommunist.org/shop

Much of the material in this pamphlet has been drawn from the newspaper of the Revolutionary Communist Group '*Fight Racism! Fight imperialism!*' and can be found at **www.revolutionarycommunist.org/americas/cuba**. Some selected articles are included in the further reading list below.

On the Cuban economy
Conceptualising Cuban Socialism
Helen Yaffe, *Fight Racism! Fight Imperialism!* 258 June/July 2017.
Brigade to Cuba: 60 years of revolution
Fight Racism! Fight Imperialism! 270 June/July 2019.
With Covid-19 under control Cuba launches new economic battle
Helen Yaffe, *Fight Racism! Fight Imperialism!* 277 August/September 2020.

On US aggression against Cuba

Socialist Cuba: old obstacles and new challenges
Helen Yaffe, *Fight Racism! Fight Imperialism!* 256, April / May 2017.
Cuba stands firm against storm of US aggression
Will Harney, *Fight Racism! Fight Imperialism!* 270 June/July 2019.
Tweets, terrorism and mercenaries, renewed attacks on Cuba
Louise Gartrel, *Fight Racism! Fight Imperialism!* 239 June / July 2014.

On Guantanamo

A close look at the Guantanamo naval base
Nuria Barbosa Leon, *Granma: official voice of the Communist Party of Cuba Central Committee*, May 2018.
Hellhole Guantanamo – outpost of imperialism
Cat Alison, *Fight Racism! Fight Imperialism!* 185 June/July 2009.

On democracy

Cuba elections: The revolution prepares for a new chapter
Will Harney, *Fight Racism! Fight Imperialism!* 263 April/May 2018.
Cuba: A political system chosen by the people
Will Harney, *Fight Racism! Fight Imperialism!* 269 April/May 2019.

On Cuban medical science

The curious case of Cuba
C William Keck and Gail A Reed, *America Journal of Public Health* 2012
Cuban medical science in the service of humanity
Helen Yaffe, *Fight Racism! Fight Imperialism!* 275 March/April 2020

On education

World Bank finds Cuban education best in Latin America and the Caribbean
Harriet Taylor, *Fight Racism! Fight Imperialism!* 241 October/November 2014
Cuban socialism: 'to be educated is to be free'
Rebecca Rensten and Helen Yaffe, *Fight Racism! Fight Imperialism!* 211 October/ November 2009

On women's rights

Obituary: Vilma Espin
Cat Alison, *Fight Racism! Fight Imperialism!* 198 August/September 2007
Supporting working mothers: Cuba's achievements bring new challenges
Rachel Francis, *Fight Racism! Fight Imperialism!* 259 August/September 2017
Cuban women lead the way in science
Cassandra Howarth , *Fight Racism! Fight Imperialism!* 266 October / November 2018

On the environment

Climate emergency- Cuba leads the way
Sam McGill and Will Harney, *Fight Racism! Fight Imperialism!* 272 October/ November 2019

On LGBT rights

Cuba. A radically different approach to trans health care
Lucy Roberts, *www.ratb.org.uk,* May 2019
Rainbow solidarity in defense of Cuba, Leslie Feinberg 2017
https://www.workers.org/book/rainbow-solidarity-in-defense-of-cuba
Socialism and equality in Cuba: The fight for LGBT rights
Cat Alison, *Fight Racism! Fight Imperialism!* 228 August/September 2012

On ALBA and internationalism

ALBA: A new dawn for Latin America.
Helen Yaffe, *Fight Racism! Fight Imperialism!* 212 December 2009 / January 2010

On the war on socialism

Troika of Tyranny: War on the struggle for socialism in Latin America
Sam McGill, *Fight Racism! Fight Imperialism!* 267 December/January 2019
The oppressed people of the world support socialist Cuba. Why doesn't the SWP?
Helen Yaffe, *Fight Racism! Fight Imperialism!* 180 August/September 2004

Published by Larkin Publications
BMC Box 5909, London WC1N 3XX

**for bulk orders please send an email to
office@rcgfrfi.plus.com to arrange payment**

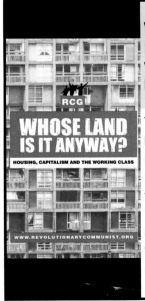